SAINT FIEND
ENEMY LINES

SAINT
BEHIND
ENEMY
LINES

OLGA KOVÁŘOVÁ CAMPORA

DESERET BOOK COMPANY • SALT LAKE CITY, UTAH

To my mom and dad,
my heroes

Library of Congress Cataloging-in-Publication Data

Campora, Olga Kovářová 1960–
    Saint behind enemy lines / by Olga Kovářová Campora.
        p.   cm.
    Includes index.
    ISBN 1-57345-227-0 (hb)
    1. Campora, Olga Kovářová, 1960–   . 2. Mormon converts—Czech Republic—Biography. 3. Mormons—Czech Republic—Biography.
    4. Mormons—United States—Biography. I. Title.
    BX8695.C22A3   1997
    289.3'092—dc21
    [b]   97-12495
                                                                CIP

Printed in the United States of America   72082

10   9   8   7   6   5   4   3   2   1

CONTENTS

ACKNOWLEDGMENTS

I express my thanks to all the courageous Czech Saints and to my many wonderful friends who helped me to grow and blossom in my understanding of God during the time of Communist darkness in Czechoslovakia. I especially would like to thank Otakar Vojkůvka, whose unique missionary approach revealed many hidden talents in myself, particularly how to work with atheistic people and those with cynical, judgmental attitudes toward God.

My deepest love and appreciation go to my wonderful parents, who always have been there for me, have believed in me, and have given me confidence. Without them I wouldn't have tried so persistently in my youth to be a good person as I searched for joyful meaning in my life.

As always, I thank my husband, Randy, who cheerfully devoted many nights to going over my manuscript and making necessary language corrections.

Appreciation goes to Sheri Dew, who challenged me to start writing this book while I was still questioning the quality of my English, and to my wonderful editor, Linda Gundry, for her uplifting, positive spirit, professional navigation, and patience in bringing the manuscript to publication.

Most of all, I am grateful to my Heavenly Father for the opportunity to be born in a country with no freedom, for he knew that the journey would bring the sweetest fruit of my life, the gospel of Jesus Christ.

1

NO HISTORY, NO HEROES

"Where are you from?" I am often asked here in the United States. Sometimes I play a geographic game by asking a question in return: "What's your best guess?" People's guesses vary a great deal—Sweden, Germany, Russia, Canada, or England. One time someone even guessed South Africa.

"Well, I am from a country which doesn't exist anymore," I reply. When I then explain that I was born in Czechoslovakia, people usually comment, "Oh, you are having a war."

"No, that's Yugoslavia," I explain. "I am from Czecho-slovakia." How close these words and countries are! Yet during the "Velvet Revolution," as the Czech revolution of fall 1989 is called, the beast of Communism was broken in my homeland—without war or bloodshed—and my country became two separate republics. Yugoslavia, however, was torn by a war that symbolizes the sore, bitter process of the gradual death of the Communist dragon in Eastern Europe. Recently I have realized what tremendous changes have occurred in the part of Europe where Communist domination, like a heavy question mark of nothingness, hung over the people for dozens of years.

When I was a small child attending elementary school, I had a strange feeling while learning about Czech history. I remarked to my parents many times, "I am living in a strange time. There has to be someone living now who is a great composer, writer, or hero. Why don't we know anything about them? There is no great history taking place now, and we don't have any heroes. Can it be possible?" They always looked sadly at me without any reply.

Indeed, I was born in a time when no news in the Czech newspapers could produce any real excitement for life. Life was filled with twisted lies from the top to the bottom, as was the news in any newspaper. And worse, these lies went beyond the walls of government and police buildings, with Communist propaganda striding boldly into the streets in the form of big, red-lettered signs and slogans: "We Will Command the Sun and the Rain!" or "With the One and Only Soviet Union for Eternity and Never Any Different." The beast of Communism strolled into movies, theaters, and shops and walked slowly but surely into the doors of people's homes. Czechs became not only disappointed and tired but gradually like walking plaster masks—emotionally exhausted and having almost no expression on their faces. That was the "permitted" public defense—passive, nonaggressive, therefore acceptable. The Czech Communists were proud of the fear they were able to so effectively produce. Fear was an unforgettable symbol of their power.

I was born in Uherské Hradiště, a small town of about 35,000 inhabitants in Southeastern Moravia, the Czech Republic, just an hour-and-a-half drive from Vienna. This area is also called Moravské Slovácko because of its close proximity to Slovakia, but the name also carries with it a unique folkloric heritage. People from Moravské Slovácko love music and dance, work endlessly in their vineyards and orchards, and are generally considered by foreigners to be the most hospitable of the Czech people.

"There is always a reason to celebrate" could easily be the principal maxim of the people there. Often you would hear the sound of the *cembalo* (a large-hammered dulcimer) so native to the region, with violins, string bass, and a clarinet. You would wonder how quickly a dinner table could be made ready for a miniature feast, just for you. The famous Czech *koláče* of apricot, prune, or poppy seed would never be missing as a dessert. Moravští Slováci are truly generous, open-hearted, giving, and jovial.

This is the place of my ancestors. I am grateful to our Heavenly Father that I was born in such a distinguished soil with such a deep, rich cultural heritage, more so since it was a shimmering heavenly gift in sharp contrast to the dark days of socialism in which I grew up. There may have been many contrary things around us and Communist elements of life that were distasteful to us, but among my people, our great heritage and the strength of our ancestral roots could serve as anchors within us. My anchor was and is the *Slovácká* music, which I love deeply. There is always sunshine in my soul whenever I listen to the sweet sound of the clarinet, violins, and bass, or the sonorous clang of the *cembalo,* my ears catching the unique rhythm and melody.

"Co Čech, to muzikant" ("Every Czech is a musician"), so the saying goes. I had a passion for musical instruments when I was small, and my first love was the old Even accordion my dad bought for me.

We had a small cabin not far from my hometown, in the middle of nature and woods, where we would go on the weekends. Close to our cabin was a large pasture where hundreds of young calves were placed each spring and summer. I always took the accordion and would go to play for the calves in the open shed. It was amazing how close they would come to me. They seemed to enjoy this "cow cultural gathering." Although my brothers thought what I did was rather on the cusp of insanity, I often saw them hiding in the woods watching how easily I could gather so many calves together, though a small number of the animals ignored my music, caring only for grass and nothing more.

Later, I fell in love with the violin, trumpet, guitar, harmonica, flute, and piano. I loved listening to all these instruments but learned to play only the piano.

"This music is my survival," I heard from many of my countrymen, who called the *Slovácko* folk music "a sweet escape from the monster." It was a safe and nonprovocative way of striking against the Communists in control of Czechoslovakia. *Šlechta*—"the barons," as we usually called the Communists and the secret police—were always somehow unsure when they saw someone happy, dancing and singing. The Communists claimed that their political system should bring people "happiness," and they didn't understand how someone could have fun or behave so happily when his or her joy didn't originate from the Communist source of thoughts and doctrines. Whatever their reasons, *šlechta* thought it intolerable to express joy publicly and openly.

"Socialism is a serious thing, you know," they would explain. "We will not tolerate any imperialistic excitement for life."

My first memories from my childhood are connected to my wonderful parents and family. My mother has often told me the story of my birth. When she was expecting me, she says that she was dreaming of a girl after two boys but thought it would be a boy anyway.

"It's a girl!" the doctor said after I was born, but my mother didn't seem to respond at all.

"Well, Mrs. Kovářová, what do you have at home so far?" he asked. She answered, "Two boys . . . ," and suddenly her tears were falling like waterfalls.

The doctor took my newborn self high in his arms and proclaimed, "To bude chytrá čiperka"—"She will be nimble and smart."

Mother always remembers this special moment of her life and says that when she heard my name, Olga Kovářová, for the first time, she felt something more beautiful than she had experienced in her life thus far. I would describe her feeling as the intense, sweet comfort of the Holy Ghost, though at the time she could not name the burning she felt within her heart.

I wouldn't change the place I grew up in. I loved our house, which was near the center of town. I thought it was paradise and couldn't think even for one second that there could possibly be a better place to live.

"Oli, where are you?" I would hear as my parents would try to find me. "Up here," I would reply from the crown of the walnut tree. I loved our garden and trees especially, because there I felt free to explore, jump, and climb.

"It is unbelievable how much strength that small girl has," I often heard my parents and neighbors say. Later in my life, my interest in physical fitness and my athletic ability would become significant parts of the path leading me, through sports, to the gospel. At the time, though, my physical strength came in handy mostly because it helped me to feel more confident whenever my older brothers tried to tease me as their younger sister.

My mom took me for swimming lessons when I was about four or five years old, as she thought I would love the water. "No, no, I don't want to do that!" I yelled, crying as if it were the end of the world. But my mom continued patiently riding the bike, with me on the front seat, along the Moravia River in my small town on our way to the lessons.

The teacher, Mr. Kulheim, was an older man, tall and slim and strict, who had built a small cabin next to the Moravia River, where he gave children's swimming lessons with his wife. He had devised an unusual teaching method, but it worked perfectly.

"It looks like a goat," I said when I saw Mr. Kulheim's equipment for the first time. Indeed, it looked rather strange. He had built a special wood "swimming apparatus," as he called it, which looked like a sawhorse with a narrow, flat piece of plywood on top. Each student individually had to lie down on his stomach so that his feet and arms were free to practice the strokes, flailing in the air.

"One hundred breast strokes," Mr. Kulheim would say as he demonstrated the swimming technique while walking around checking on us. He helped us to maintain the correct stroke and simultaneously counted the strokes faithfully.

"Are we going on the goat today?" I would ask my mom or dad when we went for another lesson. Although it seemed like small torture for some kids and even the adults, I liked this challenge and thought it was actually fun to swim on the "wooden goat."

"By the end of the course we will swim in the Moravia River," Mr. Kulheim said as I watched my mom's surprised face. "It will be the first real test of our swimming abilities."

Later I found out that this caused real anxiety for my mom and for many other parents participating in the course. People generally didn't swim in the river at all. It was terribly cold even in the hottest August and was full of mud and long river grass, not to mention its peculiar stench.

I remember how proud I was of myself while swimming in the real water of the river instead of on the wooden goat. I didn't mind the river. However, the first thing I remember after I came home that day is that my mother made sure she washed me thoroughly in the shower. "Mom, I feel like I am in a washing machine," I complained, but she knew better.

Swimming was the very first sport I started doing competitively as a seven-year-old at the elementary school. The under-appreciated dolls soon were out of sight, and instead my bedroom was shining with lots of swimming trophies.

When I was in the fifth grade, we had an art class one school morning for which we were supposed to bring some fall leaves to paint. A large and quarrelsome schoolmate, one of the biggest boys in my class, approached my desk and took my leaves from the desk right in front of my eyes. Immediately we started to fight. Surprising both myself and the rest of the class, I was able to pin the boy down to the floor. You can imagine how this experience changed my standing in the class, especially among the boys. From that time on, many of them wanted to become my friends.

"How did you do it?" asked my brothers when I told them the story after school.

"Thanks to you!" I replied to my middle brother, Zdeněk, who taught me diligently (and with a type of love only your brother can provide) by treating me to a full-nelson wrestling technique he proudly called *krajta obecná*—the universal python.

I guess I wasn't the ideal type of girl. I didn't like dolls and felt very upset when someone would give me one as a gift. I remember wondering why anybody would find it interesting to change a doll's dress or try to make her walk and sleep. I was a little bit embarrassed when I grew older and heard all the other girls' doll stories and didn't have too much to say.

"The dolls would be neatly lined up on Olga's bed," my mom recalls, "but she would be hugging a stuffed monkey under her arm while jumping in the garden." Mom knew I was a girl who loved being active, climbing, riding my bike, or just quietly sitting with a favorite book. I am grateful for a mother who understood my feelings and didn't make a big deal out of it. I suppose my being a "tomboy" was just one result of my having two brothers and being blessed with a tremendous amount of energy and health.

I love my parents and have great admiration and respect for them, because they always tried hard to find what was best for us as kids, notwithstanding all the uneasy circumstances and limited possibilities in Communist Czechoslovakia. They had experienced great pain during the war and the takeover of our country by the Communist government, but I never heard them complain, and they rarely spoke of the takeover. "It's a bitter history, but we need to move on," they would say. Although my parents couldn't guide me spiritually to become a Christian, I always looked up to them as great heroes.

My father, Zdeněk, was from a family of four children. He, his two brothers, and their father started a business literally from nothing, repairing and selling cars. The Communists came to power just at the time when the family was beginning to prosper after many years of hard work in their business.

Dad always has been described as a very hardworking, humble, and honest man. He doesn't speak too much when sitting around with other people, but he has a great gift for observation and the ability to go directly to the point when asked his opinion.

"Dad, what do you think about this?" we often asked him. He never disappointed us with his very precise judgment. He always has been straightforward in his ideas, and many times it was hard for my brothers and me to hear the truth from him.

"His precise work speaks for himself," people say of him, no matter what he is responsible for. He has a great sense of order and cleanliness. His office, his closet, and his garage always look like he has just finished cleaning and arranging them. His slogan is "It has to look like a bridegroom"—fresh and tidy and spotlessly clean. Whatever responsibility we had in the family, he would expect us to not only try our best to finish the task but to have clean hands at the end of it. "Show me your hands and I will know how perfectly you have finished your work," he would say; this is how we were passed off on any assignment around the house.

We always loved to watch him when he was doing something with his hands. His work followed a clear plan, and he wouldn't leave the place until he was completely satisfied with his final product. He loves physics and mathematics, unlike all the other members of our family. He built a complete cabin for the family without anyone else helping. It was a lot of hard work, as the cabin stands on a large hill on stony ground next to the woods.

When his oldest brother, Josef, managed to save his money and complete his university studies, it was my father's turn, as the second oldest, to save his money and begin his studies at college. This was not to be; in a very short period of time the Second World War came, and right after that, Communists took over the government and confiscated the auto shop as state property.

My mother, Dana, is the only offspring of her mother and father's marriage, though she had a half brother, Karel, from my grandfather Josef's first marriage. His first wife was Austrian, and therefore Karel moved to Vienna later on to join her.

What I always admired about my mother is her pioneer spirit. She was always able to leave old ideas behind and accept what she felt was a better outlook or a new way to live. Mom was generous, too, and never afraid to sacrifice time or whatever was necessary at the moment if she knew that the sacrifice was for something meaningful to all of us. She loved to read adventure and nature stories and was, and still is, incredibly fast in knitting Norwegian sweater patterns. Each sweater was a masterpiece, and Mom could have it done within a few days. She loved to create new patterns and play with different colors. Each member of the family had every Christmas either a new wool sweater, a hat, stockings, gloves, or a scarf. Knitting was her way of relaxing from the day's tasks. She read and knitted at the same time most of the winter evenings.

"Wow, that's beautiful! Can I see the pattern closely?" women would often ask when I wore her handmade sweaters to the grocery store, and some would even ask me for her phone number to call her and ask for the pattern.

In my mind I see my mother as a woman of action. She was engaged in some type of work at all times and always made sure we were taken care of. She has been a truly amazing example to me, though her life wasn't easy under Communism, due to her being the daughter of a former capitalist businessman. When the Communists came to power, they took all my grandparents' property. My mother was a young woman at that time. Although she earned college degrees in economics, she couldn't ever get a really suitable job, and many times manual work was all that was left. I cannot imagine how painful this undeserved punishment was for her, but she has never complained, not even to this day.

Her father, Josef Dudešek, was a pioneer in our family. Because he died long before I was born, I know him only from the stories my mom and grandma have told. However, we still speak of him often and very highly in the family, and he always seemed to me to be quite a unique man, with great magnetism towards people. As a young man, Josef was disturbed by many decisions of the Catholic church, so he changed his religion and was baptized into a Protestant faith. During Sunday mass, the local Catholic priest publicly renounced Josef as an apostate from the Catholic church, which was quite a severe punishment at the time. Some of Josef's Catholic friends turned their backs on him because of his decision.

Grandfather Dudešek started working as a shoemaker at his father's small workshop, then went on to study photography. Later on, after he married my grandmother Ludmila, he opened a shoe store and began to prosper.

Grandpa loved travel and originated a ski club in his small town, which in his time was a rarity. He loved music, photography, and especially painting. He painted with many of his friends, who helped him to learn the techniques. Most of his photographs demonstrate his great love of Slavic folklore and customs, while his paintings depict his affection for nature and the countryside.

Grandpa Josef wrote a family history in the tragic days of the Second World War. From these records, and also from the stories of other family members, I was familiar with the war tales. I knew about times when Grandpa had helped the Czech partisans with food supplies and clothes and had even hidden some of them to help in the fight against the fascists.

Also, my family described to me the very last front of the Russian army, called the Army of Marshal Malinovský, which came to "liberate" my town at the end of the war. These soldiers were criminals sentenced to death in the Soviet system, most of them taken from Siberia at the close of the war when there was no one else left to fight. The good citizens of my city had to allow Marshal Malinovský's army to enter our homes and take whatever they desired. They would come and eat all the food in the house, even the full storage supply in the basement. They took every piece of shoe leather Grandpa Dudešek had in the basement, which amounted to about five horse wagons full. They would damage the furniture and cut the pictures and paintings from the frames on the walls. These are just a few things which can be told.

When my grandparents were allowed to come back into the house, they could hardly believe what they saw. The house looked like a pigpen. You can see the knife marks on the beautiful antique pieces of furniture even today, my grandparents having left them as the only memory of wartime.

Fortunately for our family, material damage was the only scar we bore. There were many young girls in other families who suffered far worse, with soldiers taking advantage of them and causing immeasurable and never-to-be-understood damage to the soul. My grandparents had fortunately sent my mom, who was seventeen at that time, to relatives who lived in a different part of the country.

There was always a difference when my parents described their childhood. My mother had the opportunity to travel abroad as a child, experiencing great food and wonderful dresses according to the latest fashion, many social opportunities, and a good education.

My dad, on the other hand, was born to a family which didn't have much when he was a small boy. He reminded us that he and his brothers had just one pair of shoes to share together, and often instead of a hot dinner they had a sugar beet.

Yet both my parents ended up in the same boat. The war, and

especially the consequences of Communism which arrived in the forties, made them equal in their circumstances, because the Communists had taken all they possibly could from both families.

Although I was born fifteen years after World War II, the tentacles of the war deeply penetrated the lives of my countrymen. Everyone was affected somehow, and each Czech family had a sad story to tell. However, the Communist school system used the effects of the war as one of the strong weapons to show us that without the "One and Only Soviet Union," we would never have been able to live in "freedom."

I remember how I, along with my school friends, was disgusted and terrified by the countless number of "educational" movies we had to see all throughout our school years. Every other month there would be a Second World War movie which would portray the fight between the Soviets and Nazis. There is no doubt that *any* war is terrible. I can see clearly today, though, how artfully the Communists used the sad and awful effects of the war for their own ideological benefit, to build the foundation of the dauntless Soviet power. "Nothing would be possible without the great Soviet Union!"—that was how they tried to make us think.

Among the very dark, gray-colored buildings which were damaged by bullets and machine guns from the Second World War, the bullet marks left as a witness to the horrid events, I saw only the bright red colors of Russian stars. Gigantic posters of Lenin, Marx, and Brezhnev were always nearby, staring down at us. I liked only one person from this "Big Three," and that was Karl Marx, because I always thought he had a great-looking beard. Lenin bothered me with his repeating slogan, "Učit se! Učit se! Učit se!" ("Learn! Learn! Learn!") And Brezhnev? I was always afraid of him because to me he looked like a huge monkey. As a child I didn't understand any differences between socialism and capitalism, but now I can see how carefully the Communist leaders perpetrated their ideas on us already in the kindergarten.

I remember my parents telling the story of one of our neighbors, whose child was attending kindergarten. His teacher, pointing to a picture of Lenin, asked him, "Who is that?" When the boy replied, "A baldheaded man," the parents were called to the kindergarten and had to explain this "outrageous" incident. Officials could not believe that the family didn't speak grandly about Lenin in their home.

I struggled myself with the Communist slogan that "the school rears the young child instead of the family." The family was always recognized as occupying the second place, which troubled me.

Already in kindergarten the rules were rather strict. I remember that I didn't want to obey one specific rule in kindergarten, which was the nap time after lunch. We were supposed to take a nap on small reclining chairs with about twenty kids in the room. I couldn't close my eyes. "It's impossible to sleep on command!" I complained at home.

I turned from one side to the other, making a lot of noise, and I got in trouble because of that. One day I tried a different plan. When our teacher was farthest from the corner where I was "napping," I made a pianissimo humming sound: "Hummmm." In a few seconds, more classmates joined me, and in a moment the whole room was humming.

"Who is that?" the teacher asked in vain. "Everybody will sleep, is that understood?" Well, it worked for a while, and I don't remember being caught, but what I remember very well is that I went to school one day with a slip of paper from my parents, which I held as a trophy: "We will pick up our daughter Olga each day after lunch, and she will spend the rest of the afternoon with her grandmother until we return home from work." I felt relieved to know I wouldn't have to deal with nap torture again.

Another childhood memory I have about Communist oppression is connected to the political holidays. People were supposed to display both the Czech and Russian flags from their windows.

One time my dad put only a Czech flag in the window. He was immediately asked the next day by one of the Communist neighbors, "Does your family hate Russian people?"

"No," my father said, and added, "why are you asking?" The neighbor answered, "Because you don't have any Russian flags in your windows!"

I always felt that if you maintained the proper exterior and gave the correct signs to the Communist world, you would be all right and not be questioned.

Everyone was to march in the city streets on Labor Day, May 1. At that time of year, the weather was usually still cold and often rainy. The occasion was meant to celebrate the proletariat power and the freedom which came through Russia's "liberating" us at the end of World War II.

Teachers counted their students to know if all were present, since even we as children had to learn the "correct political slogan" to recite as we passed the Communist city leaders in the parade. Each member of my family had to go to the parade with his or her own group, the group to which he or she belonged at school or at work.

I will never forget coming home after four wasted hours in the parade and having hot tea and a hot dog with the family. If people were unable to go to the parade, they had to have a legitimate excuse for missing it, such as a note from their doctor. People who didn't have this were definitely in trouble, and the Communists at work would provoke them by setting up an "educational" meeting with them to find out just exactly why they were not at the parade. "Didn't you just take a day off, comrade?" (To the Communists, everyone was *comrade.*) "You are a politically immature citizen, and you should think about that," they would say in a threatening way.

Our country's Communist government knew very well why they didn't allow Czech citizens to travel from Czechoslovakia to the West: the experience would certainly open your eyes, no matter whether you were a deep-rooted Communist or someone who knew better and suffered because of Communist rule. When Communists came back from such a trip, they either criticized the obvious deficiencies of capitalism, such as unemployment, beggars on the streets, guns, crime, drugs, etc., or they behaved as if they knew more about life than any other ordinary Czech citizen. Perhaps what they really saw was simply a clearer picture of the things they were going to try to snuff out of us—happiness, initiative, freedom, and the right to stand on the street corner and say, "I believe in God."

2

QUESTIONS WITH
NO ANSWERS

I liked to be at my Grandma Ludmila's house in a small village close to Uherské Hradiště called Velehrad. I loved running through the corn and wheat fields, feeling completely free. Grandma Ludmila was the only living grandparent I had when I was eight years old, and so it was always special to be close to her.

"The head is a woman's crown" was my grandma's slogan. She loved to carefully comb my hair each morning, especially when we went to the church together.

I loved to spend whole summer vacations year after year with her. There was also another reason to be with grandma. Life in the village where she lived, and where most of my ancestors came from, seemed to me more open. It was a tiny place, like the palm of your hand.

However, in the beginning of each July it was suddenly over-run by thousands of tourists. You can imagine what this meant for a kid! It was like a fairy tale as I sat on uncountable numbers of merry-go-rounds, magic theaters, and other attractions. The Communists couldn't prevent people from gathering in the place but were especially displeased that it took place during a holy Catholic holiday. For a schoolgirl like me, the holiday was a time for fun, although we were surrounded by many visible and invisible policemen.

The village is considered a place of pilgrimage where, according to historians, the beginnings of Great Moravia were established. Archeological research has documented that Velehrad was a large city centuries ago.

You wouldn't expect the great cathedral you find in the middle of the village square. People are amazed when they see all the catacombs under the cathedral sanctuary, as well as the underground passageways. Some of these are as wide as a horse and wagon, connecting the village with prestigious castles ten kilometers away.

The other place I liked was the village cemetery. There was something so alive as I witnessed the visits of the relatives of those who had passed away. I watched how carefully they watered the flowers to keep them fresh. I spent hours walking in the cemetery in the small village during the summer, reading the names written on the tombstones, wondering about the lives of these people who had died. Soon I became a very good friend of the seventy-year-old gravedigger, and we spoke a lot about death together.

I watched many funerals and thought, It cannot be possible that this is the end and nothing else can be done. Why is it that people have goals, build houses, and live their dreams, all the while knowing that it will end one day without any continuation?

I didn't understand the Communist idea that there is nothing after this life: "Life finishes with death." I didn't like it, either.

"What would you like to eat today?" my grandma would ask, and it would be my all-time simple favorite—fresh bread with a little bit of butter and slices of fresh tomatoes on top. "Good bread is better than cake," my dad used to say. Anyone who has tasted fresh Czech bread will understand. It has a nice round or oval shape. It is heavy, with a great crust on the top and caraway seeds inside, and it has a chewy texture and an unbelievably wonderful sour taste. You can eat it without anything else and still be totally satisfied.

"Oli, you need something warm in your stomach!" Grandma used to say as she prepared some of "grandma's special." I guess most grandmothers know this kind of kitchen magic. I would refuse to eat my mom's soups, to her great disappointment, but I loved my grandma's soups. The first place I would go while I was visiting my grandma, however, would be a special basket in the kitchen cabinet where all the cookies and candies were sitting just for me. I still did it the last time I was there, last year when I went back to visit the Czech Republic, and was surprised that the old basket of goodies was waiting for me. Grandmas are special indeed!

I also remember my other grandmother, Anežka, and grandfather, Josef, my father's parents, who were still alive when I was a small child. However, I wasn't my grandma's favorite grandchild. One day she had prepared a dinner of smoked pork ribs for grandpa Josef, but I ate most of them. After that time, whenever I wanted to come to see her, she would say behind the closed door, "Nobody's home—there is a wolf here." "Well, grandma, that's not true. You are at home," I would say, but she would still only let me in on occasion. She had a lot of grandchildren, in contrast to my other grandma, and I guess she had to be on the lookout for small, curious grandchildren visitors.

My father was Catholic and my mother Protestant. As a small child I remember going to Sunday school at the Protestant church called the Evangelical Church of the Czech Brethren. I also went to the chapel with my grandma Ludmila every Sunday when I was a small child. My parents came occasionally, mostly on Christmas or Easter holidays.

One of the most significant events during the period of my early childhood was the invasion of hundreds of thousands of Russian and Soviet-satellite troops into my country on August 20, 1968. This invasion put an end to the Prague Spring, as it is called, during which some reforms had been attempted in my homeland. Russian soldiers were sent to Czechoslovakia to crush any possible attempt of the Czechs to rise up in revolution. Obviously, I didn't understand what was happening around me; I just was able to feel the emotion attached to the sweep of events. It looked to me simply like a war, because suddenly I saw hordes of Russian soldiers in my small town, riding their tanks, drunk almost all the time, and behaving like we the Czechs were the visitors and they were the home team. It was the very first time in my life when I wore the Czech tricolors of blue, white, and red on my lapel. I felt very proud of my Czechness.

During those months I spent a lot of time with my grandmother Ludmila, as I remember, listening to the latest reports over the radio. I remember my grandma standing in her small living room with me while we sang the national anthem together. As she cried, she looked into my eyes and said, "Oli, we might have a war and we might not. Let's kneel down and pray together." I didn't understand the meaning of the war, but because I had heard so much about the Second World War from TV, the movies, and from what my parents and grandparents had told me about it, I immediately knelt down and was ready for prayer. After the prayer, Grandma said, "Now we know we will be in the hand of the Lord, whatever happens."

During this critical time in my country's history, we tried to live our lives as normally as was possible. As usual on Fridays, we drove to our cottage in the woods in Salaš, which was just about thirty minutes from our house. To get to the cottage we drove down a road with lovely trees and woods on both sides. Everything was normal until we were stopped by a company of Russians near a clearing. After we were ordered out of the car, they searched every corner of it. When one of them found my father's small transistor radio, a fight ensued over the question of who among them would be the sole possessor of the bounty. In the trunk of the car was my small bicycle, which I often brought to the cottage. One of the soldiers pulled it from the trunk, put it on the road, and started to ride it. I was upset, indeed, but when we saw what a hard time the soldier had just to stay up on two wheels, it became obvious he had never ridden a bicycle before. He ended up in the bushes. I lost my bicycle, but at least this part of the story made the family laugh later about our sorry encounter with the Russian troops.

These experiences had an impact on me, so much so that I had quite a hard time at school when we had to begin to study a second language. Of course you can guess what it was: Russian. Every child studied the language from the sixth grade until the end of high school, and many continued at the university as well. When I heard the language, it brought back to me all those unpleasant memories.

Most of the Russian language teachers had a proper "profile," and most of them were members of the Communist party; therefore they took the language very seriously—really to the point of its being a political class instead of just a class for learning a new tongue. The other group of Russian language teachers were those who were forced to teach Russian as a punishment for some mistaken thought or deed, or perhaps they were simply assigned to that job and didn't have a choice. I had a few of the teachers from this latter group, and learning Russian from those teachers was definitely a relief for me and the rest of the class. With the former group of teachers, everyone was more stressed with fear than in math class, with the exception of those who belonged to the politically prestigious group of the class. A bad grade might mean that you just were not good at the language, but it could also signify that you were trying to sabotage the class. It all depended on how the teacher took it.

By the end of high school (called *gymnasium* in Europe), students were given a huge final exam which was called *Maturita*. They were tested in four subjects: mathematics, Czech language, the subject which was going to be the student's major field in the university or technical college in the future, and Russian language. After so many years of learning Russian, most students could speak almost fluently, particularly since Russian is a Slavic language like Czech (with the exception that Russian uses the Cyrillic alphabet while Czech uses the Roman). However, few students were actually proud of their knowledge of Russian. It was a forced education, something we were required to know, and we hated it deeply because of the whole political and social impact the Soviet Union had on the life of the people in our country.

I did feel attached to religion as a child. It was because I sensed a different feeling and order inside the chapel, in comparison to in the school or on the street. Sunday school lessons usually taught us about Jesus, though I understood and respected him more as a historical person than as deity. Although I didn't understand the meaning of spiritual things I was taught in the Sunday school at that time, there was a natural feeling inside me to form a bond with religion and ideas about God.

When I entered the third grade at the elementary school, we had to fill out a paper and say if we attended any church. I wrote, "Yes, the Protestant church," as did a few others in the class. I saw the scorn in my teacher's face, and from some of the other children as well, when all of the church-going children had to stand up in the class.

I asked myself suddenly, and probably for the first time in my life, "Is there something wrong with the fact that I go to church?" I couldn't comprehend at that age what it was that bothered me about that steely gaze on the faces of my schoolmates, but I remember thinking about it and telling my mom about the experience, trying to figure out one of my first "losses" in the eyes of my schoolmates.

I was eight years old at that time. The older I became, the more frightened I was to publicly declare that I believed in God and attended church.

In the fifth grade, when we had a lesson about religion, our

teacher displayed on the blackboard a large poster with one of
Marx's famous ideas—"Religion is the opiate of the people!" It
was a painful feeling, like being a defendant in court, as I saw my
teacher laughing in front of the class and proclaiming that "only a
blockhead could believe in God in today's modern world!"

For a growing child to hear these ideas created a great amount
of controversy in my mind, and feelings of embarrassment which
grew worse without any decent place to discuss questions regarding
God. Naturally I wondered about his existence. On the other hand,
the majority of young people stopped caring about the topic at all.
They felt it was not worthy to discuss because they knew the
answer from the school lessons, and thus it affected their morals
and the way they cared about each other. "Slowly but surely a
repeated lie becomes truth." That was and still is a Czech saying
that describes the state of mind of many Czech citizens during the
Communist years.

I did question the existence of God. I don't think I became
more and more skeptical about God, but I felt truly frightened to
do anything with these thoughts of mine. My religious feelings
slept inside me for a long period of time before they were gradually awakened. Deep inside, I believed God existed, but I didn't
give it any other further thought or pondering. In those years, all
the things we were taught at school, no matter what the subject,
were designed to attack and uproot the idea of religion.

I never laughed at the very small number of courageous children who openly admitted that their whole family went to church.
Usually, these were children of priests or members of an openly
rebellious, anti-Communist family.

As for my family, we didn't go to church at all during a certain
period of time. I was probably the only one in the family who continued to attend, and then only on outings with my grandma.

The political atmosphere in my country in the seventies was
opposed to religion with such hostility that if the school found out

you attended any church and that you had desires to study at the university level, your application would simply be rejected. You would pass all the hard exams, and then the university would write you a letter: "You have successfully passed all the exams, but because of the high number of candidates you are not admitted. Good luck to you in the future!"

It was important for the Communists to have a future generation with, as they put it, "the correct political and philosophical profile." If you didn't fit that profile, you had very little chance of gaining a higher education.

Even during the years when my parents didn't attend any church, they taught us one family rule: "Always be honest with others." One day I went to my piano lesson, after practicing very little that week, and I knew my performance would be very poor. I put a bandage on my finger and told my young piano teacher that I could not play that day, explaining that I had cut myself.

"Well, can I see your finger?" she asked.

I took off the bandage very slowly, wanting at that moment to be anyplace but there. She looked, and there was my completely healthy-looking finger. I felt awful about myself. The teacher asked my mother to come to school and talk to her. "Frankly, Mrs. Kovářová, I would never expect anything like that from Olga. She has disappointed me greatly," the teacher said in front of me. I felt terribly guilty when I heard these words and spent the whole afternoon crying in the bathroom.

"Come here," my mother said as she came to free me from the bathroom, and then she took me in her arms. I appreciated the fact that my parents didn't try to make the situation more painful, but instead they asked, "Why did you do it?"

I had a long talk with them about the piano lessons. My teacher, new to the school, was a talented young pianist and was more adventurous in challenging her students than other teachers had been. I felt so overwhelmed by the amount of music she assigned to us that sometimes I felt like giving up.

Although my mom talked to her about my motives in the bandage incident, my teacher was rather cold to me for a period of some months. I would just go to my piano lessons, do my assignments, and leave the class. The lessons were very quiet, with only the minimum of words needed, without any expression on the teacher's face.

I started to practice more diligently. After a few months, I was chosen for a recital. After my performance, my teacher came to me and said, "It was great, Olga." I looked at her and knew immediately that she had forgiven me.

Ms. Chmelařová stayed on as my piano teacher for the next seven years, and we became very good friends.

"She isn't teaching here anymore," they told me later. How sad I was when one day I learned she had been transferred to another school because she believed in God. The school found out that she was a member of some religious group. Unfortunately, I never found out which one because she just disappeared. She was accused of talking to her students about God. It was true; during the piano lessons, we had a lot of discussions about God. But I was grateful for them. I have continued to search for her because I am indebted to her for a love of the piano and for her help in keeping my interest in God alive.

3

GYMNASIUM DAYS

What's wrong with all my beginnings? I have asked myself many times. Most of my starts have been very painful for me. However, this way I have learned many times to see new angles of myself—sometimes surprising and fulfilling bits of wisdom.

My high school years began with embarrassment and disappointment. By the end of the ninth grade of the elementary school, I had chosen to continue at a *gymnasium,* the European equivalent of four years of college-preparatory high school. To be admitted to the gymnasium, I had to pass an exam in Czech language and mathematics. I was fine with Czech, but I had a very hard time in mathematics. I felt terrible when a professor came to tell our group exactly which of us did not pass. It was a bitter feeling to hear among the few names my very own. My body shrunk down into the school bench and I closed my eyes. "What am I going to do now?" I thought hopelessly. "What will I tell my parents?"

"The additional oral exam is scheduled for this afternoon, and all the students whose names were read a minute ago will remain in the class," the professor continued. I felt condemned. I watched many of my schoolmates walk out happily and in triumph from the class, yet a few of us were sitting in the benches like nails driven into the wood.

The additional mathematical exam was longer than both morning exams put together. There were four mathematics professors in attendance and an endless number of mathematical problems. While I wrote on the blackboard and explained step by step what I would do to solve each assigned problem, I was amazed at what I heard from myself. My voice was calm, and I went from one solved problem to the next. It was a piece of cake this time.

"Well, Olga, you really did great this afternoon, and there is no reason you shouldn't be accepted to study here," the head professor of the mathematical committee pronounced.

I left the office and my blue dress was marked with the chalk all over, but I felt so good—like a miner who can see a light after a long day in the coal mine and doesn't care about coal dust. I wondered for weeks and months after this experience how it was possible for me to pass the additional oral exam with such an extraordinary peace in my mind. Frankly, when I walked out of the office, I remember that I was more amazed and surprised than the professors.

The beginning of my study at the gymnasium was very, very hard. Moreover, after a few months we got a new professor for physics. To my disappointment, it was the same school teacher I had had at the elementary school for math. She was a very moody and choleric type of teacher, and if she didn't like a particular student she knew how to give him or her a really hard time. By the end of the first half of the year I had a grade of 4 from physics, which is a "D" in the American grading system. Not only one 4, but also another one in Russian language, and my other grades weren't so hot either.

The Russian professor was muscular, heavy-set, with hair that made her look like a water goblin. However, she was a very powerful woman in her mid-fifties, a member of the Communist party's head committee at the school. We called her the Red Goblin. She stepped on everyone's neck with nonsense tasks which most of the time didn't have anything to do with Russian language but always with Soviet politics. She forced us to buy the Russian newspaper *Pravda* for every class and to read it from top to bottom, then give a report in the class. This happened four times per week. Whenever she taught us about any Russian writer or poet she would relate him or her to some Communist ideological point. I developed a dislike for the Russian language, and I spent as little preparation for the class as possible.

I was greatly relieved when we finally got a new professor in the beginning of the second year. He was young and looked like he had just been released from prison because of his very short haircut. However, he actually taught the topic we were supposed to be learning, which was Russian literature, and very quickly I fell in love with a number of Russian authors: Tolstoy, Dostoyevsky, Chekov, and many others. Even more, I was able to improve my grade to an A. Grades were so tricky and unpredictable in our Communist-run schools when just one professor was exchanged for another.

Another difficult reality I faced in the beginning of my high school years was that there was a completely new group of young people around me in the class. Students were from a different part of town and from villages which belonged to our town's school district. I saw how almost everyone turned suddenly very serious about school. It was a painful transition from elementary school. I felt as if I were on a windmill without any time to look back or forward. It was like running water between my fingers or like riding a roller coaster for the first time. There were so many different ideas running through my head, from great excitement to a captivating and magnetic fear. Looking back, I realize that almost everyone felt the same as I did, but in the beginning we didn't know each other and were so scared that everyone thought, " Oh, that's just me. There is something wrong with me."

Above all, some professors made school even harder with their demanding warnings: "You have to realize that life begins now. It's gymnasium! Wake up!" "You aren't at the elementary school," professors would say when a student's habits appeared to be immature. Nevertheless, there still existed a small number of professors, especially young ones, who didn't seem to relish contributing to the nightmare.

Today, looking back, I can see that much of the unpleasant awkwardness, the paralyzing tension in and out of the class, originated from our teachers' relentlessly pushing us into an adult Communist world and our consequent self-doubt and worries about our future. We as students could sense how certain professors stood in fear of other professors. It was easy to figure it out, because if someone was a member of the Communist party, all the other students, professors, and even the janitor had to watch out for them. We had a saying used on a daily basis in the Communist times: "Weigh your words!" It meant that everyone had to watch carefully what he or she said in front of the Communists.

During the first two years of gymnasium I went to the Tuesday night meetings of the Protestant Youth at the church in which I had been baptized as a small child and where I had regularly attended with my grandma during my childhood. Only my parents knew I attended these meetings, however; Communist teachers and community leaders would persecute anyone who was openly religious.

The church where I attended youth meetings had a small parsonage, which was an old two-story house. The priest, a favorite among the members, was transferred, and in his place came a younger family who lived there with a young man who was planning to study theology. I remember some members telling me that Communists made the change with the purpose of reducing attendance at the church services.

The Tuesday meetings consisted of a very small group of teenagers and university students, probably about eight of us or so. The room was constantly cold, both in winter or summer, and dark—not inviting at all. We discussed scriptures, mostly from the New Testament. Most of the time it was not a real study but rather a repetition of the history of Christ. Attending a meeting was like trying to meditate on God in an environment of total personal fear.

I had a lot of questions about all the miracles that Jesus performed. The way they were explained didn't satisfy me, and neither did it bring me the spiritual passion to dig deeper. At that time a story about the Savior seemed just a piece of information or perhaps a fairy tale, no more or less. It was hard for me as a teenager to make any headway with my questions about God. I felt I could not explore my faith because of my lack of knowledge about God. "Is it wrong to question God?" I asked myself. But what should I have done when I had questions which were not meant to destroy my belief in him but to discover him?

I felt that each of my unanswered questions was like an icicle hanging on the side of a house, and from that icicle came only a small drop of water when the sun came out for just a second. Something inside me told me there had to be more to Christ than had been taught to me. However, I didn't know how to get all the water from the icicles. I don't remember having any real spiritual feelings of the Holy Ghost. But I don't think I had even an intellectual idea of what inspiration would have felt like had it come.

Christ's love was the only teaching I could relate to, due to the level of my understanding at that time. I did not understand the idea of fearing God. This felt too similar to the fear everyone had of the Communists. In me this fear became a negative, destructive fear which stopped me from exploring my faith.

I went to the meetings and enjoyed being with this small church group of young people until the day that I found out that a boy in the group was in love with me. I didn't like him at all, and I protected myself by not going to the classes anymore. I completely stopped going to church meetings during my third year of gymnasium. From that time on, I had only occasional encounters with someone on a religious topic, but as I recall it was always a very flat exchange of a few ideas, with both sides too confused to come up with anything meaningful.

Even friendships were somehow affected by the existing regime. We had dancing lessons in the second year of gymnasium. All the students were to attend, as it was part of any gymnasium's curriculum to learn social etiquette and dancing. I loved to dance, so I always enjoyed this class. I had a good dance partner named Tonda (Tony) and it was wonderful to learn dance steps, starting with the polka and ending with the rumba and tango. It took one whole semester to take these classes, and by then Tonda and I knew we liked each other.

By coincidence, my father worked with Tonda's, but there was a slight difference between them. His father was a Communist and mine wasn't. As I learned later, Tonda's father didn't like my dad at all and was very angry at his son for being attracted to me. Tonda himself told me many times that his father insisted that he quit dancing with me—the daughter of a non-Communist. Tonda laughed and was happy to do just the opposite of his father's will. However, I learned that Tonda's personality was nice but very differently oriented from the standards of my family.

I remember how shocking it was for me when at the very last dancing lesson, where we were supposed to exchange small gifts, I received from him a small book of love poems. On the first page were written these words, which froze me: "Live in such a way that everybody will be envious of you! Your Tonda." This one phrase aptly described the motto of Communists, as they tried to live above everyone else. It changed my feelings about him immediately, and both fathers were very happy when in a few weeks this ideologically contradicting relationship was ended. Soon another girl replaced me.

There were a few activities which formed my personality during the teenage years. I continued with my piano studies, practiced a number of sports, and loved reading biographies. I realized during my gymnasium years that I often felt more comfortable in adult company than among my schoolmates.

I was involved in many different sports, from swimming to track, the long jump, fencing, canoeing, orienteering, gymnastics, handball, skiing, hiking, and many others. It was easy to find me because I was almost always in the sport hall practicing either fencing, swimming, or distance running. These were the three I did most of the time.

Sports helped me achieve a degree of balance between body and mind. I especially liked doing sports for competition, because as I prepared myself to compete, I went through many specific practice routines and could see my own improvement. I loved the feeling of being able to overcome my own old limits and reach farther in my physical abilities. I always felt a great amount of joy as I participated in sports events. Although it might sound strange, I do believe that that was one of many gentle ways Heavenly Father taught me to feel the influence of the Holy Ghost, as I reached a finish line or gave the last direct hit in fencing after long minutes of tactics and strategies. It was a kind of joy which didn't focus only on the excitement of winning but also on my happiness at overcoming the old person inside me and at consciously participating in becoming someone new. In those moments as the heart was pumping vigorously, I felt always more capable of accomplishing many other goals which didn't have any direct link to sports— school work, piano lessons, and choosing what kind of book to read, which friendships to cultivate, and which leisure activities to select.

Sports taught me its own unique physical discipline. I learned about my body's abilities and how to have control over myself—I learned the body was my helper.

Because I was growing up in a small Communist town, the opportunities to choose different hobbies or any kind of more specific activities were very slim and limited. This is another reason I chose sports. I loved the variety it offered. Also, the focused physical activity kept me from doing wrong. I could see many of my schoolmates involved in smoking, drinking, dating unwisely, and attending questionable disco clubs, then sometimes getting married too young due to unwanted pregnancy.

The older I became in my teenage years, the bigger gap I felt between myself and a majority of my schoolmates. I didn't feel comfortable in all their weird activities, which they seemed to enjoy quite naturally. Somehow I was always looking for an adult friend. As a matter of fact, I became very good friends with my gymnasium music professor, a young woman who had just finished her master's degree and had started teaching at our gymnasium. Because of her influence I started singing in the school choir and also performed on piano, going to many high school competitions.

Almost every weekend I competed in track or fencing. In track, I trained for the 400- and 800-meter distance races. The 400 meters had to be run just like 100 meters, even though it was four times as long. It was the most challenging track event for me, both physically and mentally. I had to plan very carefully my physical tactics, because by the end of the four hundred meters, every meter seemed a hundred.

Actually, I myself hadn't chosen to learn fencing. In sixth grade, one of my schoolmates convinced me to join. Out of about fifteen of us who started the same class, by the end of the second year I was the only one who had continued in fencing. I liked the fact that fencing was very different from other sports. We learned specific moves with our feet, from a simple push forward and a push back to specific fencing steps such as *patinando* and *balestro,* as well as working on basic concentration. We had to train the legs and arms separately for a long period of time before we got a sword, and for women it was only a foil.

Fencing was rather an unusual sport for a girl, but what I really liked about it and why I stayed interested was that this sport not only required my muscles but my mind as well, along with the ability to concentrate and create action and strategies on my own. That was different from distance running.

I became successful in the local fencing matches at first, and then in the more important matches on the national level. Later on, I was competing even with foreign fencers and therefore was involved in serious training and competitions. However, after a certain period of time, I began to feel sharp pains in my hip. The sport physician recommended that I quit competing and do fencing just for fun. I decided immediately that this would be the best thing for me, although I was very disappointed to have to end my career in the sport. I went through physical therapy and thought that I might really like to become a physician myself. I was nearing the end of my studies at gymnasium and had to decide what I was going to study at the university.

4

DETOUR

I didn't like my teenage years. I found myself not too comfortable among my schoolmates. I was always a leader type of person, and adults frequently put me in the position of leading the group. This was painful for me at the high-school level; I knew that I didn't fit in with the normal crowd. In addition, I always seemed to be searching for something, though I did not know what. I would spend hours in the library, reading different philosophers' ideas about life. I looked into the books nobody else would read. I was amazed by *The Resurrection* by Tolstoy and by the extraordinary work of Albert Schweitzer, R. Rolland, Goethe, and others. I tried to write, to compose music on the piano. I tried my hand at painting. I felt that I wanted to do something extraordinary with my life. Something inside of me caused me to look for a way to spend my life doing something meaningful for others.

As a teenager I could see that I lived in a society where certain people were privileged just because of their belonging to the Communist party. I couldn't understand completely why restrictions and rules were so solidly concrete for a non-Communist, but incredibly flexible for the Communists. In complete accordance with their will, nothing or everything could happen. I didn't know how to act without a solid understanding of the ideas of God and religion. It was natural that as a teenager I would have questions about right and wrong. Teenagers often look for principles of truth that work in all of life's instances, without any exception. I asked myself, Why do I have to be good when I can see that there are so many other people who are bad, and they have more of life's privileges than good people? Why do some people undeservedly suffer, and on the other hand, why do so many bad people seem to get what they want? If there is a God, why do people experience wars, illnesses, suffering, and injustice? Why, if God really exists, does he allow all this, when according to religious teachings, he is so loving?

The worst part of being reared not in a healthy religious environment but among Communist atheists, who laughed at any concept that life might continue after death, was that people generally became passive, uninterested in discussing or considering the meaning of life. I saw the effects this education had in our Communist-dominated society, with its strong anti-religious force and the constant threat of persecution for those with religious feelings. I began to notice that people's fear took away their hope of finding happiness and replaced productive conversation and exchange of thought with sterility. People became involved in theft, alcoholism, divorce, manipulation, lies, dishonesty, and ever-increasing unhappiness.

There were a few experiences during my teenage years where I could see how close I was to getting on the wrong path. In our neighborhood, there was a girl my age who attended the same gymnasium as I, and we became friends. She was very interested in the Beatles, and her boyfriend was a disc jockey in a local dance club. She invited me to come along with some of her friends to this dance club. There was one strict rule to get a ticket: You had to be at least sixteen years old. Even in this place there were a lot of members of the secret police. Although they tolerated our dancing to music with English lyrics, apparently they were worried about young people's enthusiasm for music from western Europe and the US. Later I found out from friends that the disc jockey was working for the local secret police, and the music he generally played was a collection of records that had been confiscated at the borders from Western Europeans entering our country.

The dance club I went to was opened for high school students twice a week from eight to ten o'clock in the evening. Although alcoholic beverages were permitted only for those eighteen years and older, the waiters, happy to make extra money, sold the alcohol to everyone. Within one hour or so, I noticed that some of the young people weren't able to dance because they were drunk. I liked the dancing part of going to the club, however, and was always anxious to learn a new type of dance. It didn't mean anything romantic to me—just enjoyment of movement. Probably the worst aspect of my going to the dance club often was that it brought me into contact with a number of young people who had few moral values. My friend from the gymnasium, in fact, fell into worse and worse situations after we parted company, and she eventually ended up first as a youthful unwed mother, then later as a bitter, unhappy adult.

One of my passions during high school was traveling—generally in the form of hitchhiking, which is very common in my country. I traveled with a high school girlfriend thorough Poland one whole summer, seeing the country from the south to the north. As everyone knows, this form of traveling is not the safest. One terrifying incident completely discouraged me from hitchhiking forever.

It was a sunny summer day during our school vacation, and my friend Věra and I decided to travel to one small city close to our town. We were hitchhiking, when suddenly a very strange car pulled over, which had big plastic bags instead of glass windows. It should have occurred to us that the car had been broken into.

Inside, there were three almost bald young men who offered to take us. I didn't like the idea and told Věra I was not going. She asked, "Why? What's wrong with you?" I told her I just didn't feel comfortable. We had a small discussion while the men were trying to encourage us to go. " Olga, don't be wimpy. If you don't go, I'll go by myself. Bye." Before I could respond, she was already sitting in the car.

I joined her in the car, though I still felt very uncomfortable. Immediately I noticed an empty liquor bottle on the floor and could see that the men were slightly drunk. The driver could hardly see anything through the plastic bags and was driving very fast. There was a small hole, just a couple of inches wide, in the plastic bag.

"This isn't right. This isn't right," I whispered to Věra.

"I know now," she said. The first surprise came after a few minutes, when the driver turned in a completely opposite direction from where we wanted to go.

"Where are you going? Stop here; we want to go in the opposite direction," I said.

"Oh, we just need to drive couple of kilometers to take care of a small business and we'll get back on the road," one of them told me.

"What are we going to do?" I asked Věra.

"We have to try get out as soon as possible," she replied. The men didn't talk to us much, but from their faces it was obvious that there was some plan in their minds.

Giving the excuse that I needed to use the restroom, I sat tensely as the men drove into the small town, apparently a town with which they weren't familiar. They drove around a bit, obviously irritated. One of the men pointed to a shopping center and we drove around to the loading dock in the back of the shopping center. Two of them jumped from the car and took a box of some goods.

Now we were certain we had fallen into dangerous company.

Again we insisted that we needed to take a brief break. The men hesitated, but finally one of them got out of the car. With him following our every step, my friend and I went into a grocery store and bought a sandwich, then insisted on finding a restroom. With our angry guard following, we walked inside the shopping center and entered a dentist's office on the second floor. As we walked in, I knew that was the only place in the mall where he wouldn't follow us. Too many people sitting around, just watching each newcomer arrive. A few dentists looked strangely at us.

"We need an emergency exit; we are being followed," I said, almost breathless.

"Here it is," said one of the nurses as she opened the door, and in a few minutes we were outside of the office and away from the man.

My friend apologized for getting us both into this mess, and we decided to find the nearest bus home. As we walked along the road trying to find a bus stop, we saw the strange car rapidly approaching us. We plunged into a cornfield with tall stalks to hide us from our pursuers. We were certain by now that they had some evil plan in mind for us. We held our breath as the dark blue car raced along the road toward us—and then sighed with relief as the men drove away without stopping.

Finally a bus came by and stopped for us. We enjoyed a wonderful feeling of safety as we boarded it, and we expressed our relief to each other that the incident had not ended more tragically. We also promised each other never to hitchhike again. We found a couple of days later in the newspapers that these three men were fugitives from Ostrava city prison and that they had been caught by the police in Slovakia.

I have thought many times about this experience, and I know it was the Holy Ghost who prompted me not to get into the car in the first place. I don't know what would have happened if I hadn't gone with my friend once she had hopped into the car; she might have escaped, and she might not. She was always a little less fearful and more eager to experience any kind of danger than I was. We remained friends for some time, but Věra was really a much greater adventurer than I was, and I had to say no a few times until eventually she may have felt I was a coward. Later she found a boyfriend, a schoolmate of ours, and we went our separate ways.

When the fourth year of my studying at the gymnasium came, I had to decide, along with all other students, what type of study I would choose for my future. I filled out my application for the university in Brno and started to prepare for all the exams we were supposed to take. I knew that my parents weren't members of the Communist party and that one of my grandparents had been pronounced a capitalist by the local Communist leaders. However, I still hoped this would not affect my decision to study at the university. The exams went just fine, but within a month I was heartbroken to read the official word on my college admission: "Due to the high number of candidates you are not accepted at Brno University." I appealed the university's verdict but still didn't get accepted, with the same reason cited as in the first letter.

I didn't know what to do, and my parents didn't know how to help me. For a time we all felt pretty hopeless. I applied for a job at an elementary school in a village close to my hometown. I knew that I would have to help myself. My parents could give me moral support but couldn't perform any miracles for me. I made a strong resolution that I would find a way to get to the university the next year, and that I would search high and low to find a way to be accepted. There had to be a way to do it. The most discouraging part of the whole experience was the fact that I saw other schoolmates who were accepted at the most prestigious universities in the country despite their poor grades. The parents of these students were Communists. This made me really upset and created the heat of resentment in me. These schoolmates just laughed at those of us who were rejected "due to the high number of applicants," knowing full well the reality of the sentence.

"Are you so naive that you don't know that all you need is some good Communist who will back you, so that you can be accepted at a university?" a few other friends said. I came home and discussed this with my parents, but my father told me, "Nothing like this can be worthy of any Kovář child. That's a dirty way to start your life—you will be the same as all the rest of the Communists."

"But, Dad, I really want to go study."

"Then you have to try harder and get the best results," he said.

"How is it possible that a number of students who had the poorest grades were accepted, and yet another number of us, no matter how great our grades are, weren't accepted?"

"I don't have any answer for that," he replied sadly.

I started working at the elementary school. In the office next to mine was a new teacher who had just finished her studies at the same university to which I was applying. She had earned her master's degree in physical education and geography. I was helping her with her classes, and we soon became good friends.

"Well, you really do have a great talent in athletics. What if you change your mind and apply at the university as a student of physical education?" she said. "I think you really could succeed. You are pretty good in fencing, and you have been competing on the national level. I think I might have some good advice for you."

"What is that?" I asked.

"That it would be good to apply for a major in physical education because of your great achievement on the national level, and that you could combine those studies with a subject which would please the Communists so that they could see that you are interested in their politics," she concluded.

"Do you mean that I would have to apply to study the Marxist-Leninist philosophy?" I asked her, shocked.

"It doesn't have to be directly philosophy. Do you remember the subject of citizen education at the elementary school and at gymnasium?" she asked.

"Yes, the most boring and painful classes I have attended in my life."

"Well, you can apply for that," she said with a serious face.

"Are you kidding? That's absolutely impossible. Everybody would laugh at me."

"Olga, you have to be realistic. You have to take a detour to get where you want to be; otherwise you don't have any chance. Do you get it?" she said, looking directly into my eyes. "You want to study, don't you?"

"Yes," I replied.

"Well, think about it. If you find a better way, let me know. But believe me, I just came from the university and I know the circumstances there. I am your friend. I don't want to make a fool of you. I want to help you because you are a focused, committed, talented, and good person. It would be a shame to see you end up somewhere without the education you desire. You just have to take different steps to achieve your goals."

Angry and confused, I came home and discussed the whole matter with my parents. How would this new plan make me feel about myself in the future? How should I deal with the obstacle of an unjust political system in such a way that I wouldn't have to bend the spine of my character and become another victim of the sterile society into which I was born?

Even my parents didn't know exactly what was best to do, because I was the only one of their children who had decided to study at the university. They themselves had experienced major disappointments with the Communist government, which changed many of their dreams. Although my dad eventually finished his college studies while he worked at his regular job, he couldn't get the work he wanted most; he was told that he wasn't politically

committed enough to public life. Well, there was only one category
of people who were "committed"—the Communists.

I felt glad that my parents had chosen to be honest no matter
how confused and unjust the Communist society was, but I also
saw that they were very reluctant to interfere in any way that would
force them to act on the edge of danger—that is, to go either with
or against the Communists. Moreover, the Communists liked it
when people were pressed to act against them. Like professional
actors, they excelled at creating a scenario. Then they brought ordinary people onstage and provoked them into action, waiting for
these victims like hungry hyenas who would go for any piece of
food. It was one of their ways of showing how powerful the
Communist system was. To catch families in some trap, the local
Communists would ruin the most vulnerable member of that family. It wouldn't necessarily mean the sudden repression of the family right away, but perhaps when the child would apply for school
or the father for a better and more responsible job, suddenly the
unbelievable rumor would start and the Communists would remind
the family of some of their "sins" from the past. Everyday life was
like skating on very thin ice. We Czechs never knew where the trap
was being prepared for either everyone to be caught in, or only for
one person the Communists would pick on for some nonsensical
reason.

I was eighteen years old and belonged to the part of society that
the local Communists would keep a sharp eye on and watch our
actions, so that there could be a "proper" reaction from their side.
Apparently I needed to be properly punished, as well as my parents, for the actions of my grandparents, who were "artful bour-
geois thinking only about themselves," as the Communists defined
those who had prospered in the capitalist days in Czechoslovakia.

The more I discussed my future school possibilities, the more I
realized that I would have a chance at education only if I took the
suggested "detour."

"Once you are in school, you can switch to a different field of study," my friend at the elementary school told me. I filled out the application, choosing as my major fields of study physical education and civic education. The application didn't look like mine—I felt that I was writing it for someone else. I sent it to the university, and they sent me all the requirements for the entrance exam, which I was to take six months later.

I practiced all the different sports, and actually I enjoyed that a lot. Even my attitude changed, and I looked forward to the exam. However, I didn't enjoy preparing for the exam for the civic education studies. I couldn't believe what kind of Communist ideological and philosophical garbage they required a person to know for the exam! I couldn't count how many times I just threw the textbooks into the corner in disgust. How could I possibly benefit from these lies and the nonsense written in these textbooks? If someone had told me I could somehow benefit from this, I certainly would not have believed them. However, when I later became a member of the Church, I realized what a strong weapon I had in my hands, and a certain scripture became very meaningful to me: "Behold, I send you forth as sheep in the midst of wolves: be ye therefore wise as serpents, and harmless as doves" (Matthew 10:16). But at the time, before I knew that the Lord had a plan for me, I felt angry to be forced to study Communist philosophy.

I passed my exams with the highest marks and got a letter from the university within a few weeks informing me of my admittance. My parents were so happy for me that I was actually surprised at how many tears it brought to their eyes. I realized that they could hardly believe that I could succeed despite my "bad" capitalist background.

I brought the letter to my friend at the elementary school, and she was excited for me. A few months later she told me that her dad was a very close friend of the dean of the physical education department at Brno University and that he had mentioned my name to his friend before I went to the exam so that my application wouldn't "fall through the cracks." I knew her father, and I knew that he was a very honest man, a professor at one of the local high schools, admired for his hard work with the young people of the city.

"Does it mean that I wouldn't have been admitted to the university?" I asked my friend.

"Well, Olga, you just needed a hand which would put your university application on the right side of the table. My dad did it for you because he knows you and your wonderful parents," she continued. When she saw my confused face, she added, "Olga, don't worry, because you worked very hard to succeed on your own. You were admitted because you really deserved it. My dad didn't do anything but to make sure that your application wouldn't be put in the garbage before the admissions committee could grade your real abilities and talents. That's all."

CHAPTER

5

UNIVERSITY LIFE

I lived with my parents until I was accepted to the university at the age of nineteen. From my many visits in the past, I was familiar with Brno, the second largest city of Czechoslovakia, where I would be living throughout my university studies. However, to live in the city as a university student was a completely different world for me. Suddenly, I had to become a fully independent person, responsible for my own future. Brno seemed to have a cold spirit and not much personality in comparison with my small hometown. I felt I had to try hard to make my own mark and get in touch with the heart of the city. I was happy to be here but also felt very lonely. For the first time in my life, I was without my family and on my own.

"Will you go with us for a couple of beers?" my new school-mates asked me the very first day of school.

"Sorry, I don't drink beer," I replied.

"Oh, well, then you should learn very fast, girl. Beer is the heart of being a healthy student at the university." They laughed and started walking towards the closest pub. I started to follow them, but when I stepped into the pub, I turned my face in disgust from the cigarette smoke and the drunken spirit there.

I did make a good contact with the students in my study group at school, but after-school activities seemed very strange to me from the beginning. I wasn't used to going directly from school to the pub. My fellow students told me there was something wrong with me if I did not want to join them.

"Come on, Olga. You can at least have a lemonade, can't you? Or do you just want to ignore your friends?" Occasionally I would go with them, but I was always in a hurry to finish my lemonade and go directly to my dormitory and take a shower. I couldn't stand the obtrusive, nasty pub stink in my clothes and in my hair. In my social life at the university, I often felt I was fighting to stay clean and wholesome. "Is this what I wanted?" I would ask as I looked in the shower mirror.

I loved physical education. The introduction to the Marxist-Leninist philosophy, on the other hand, was a real burning hell. We discussed a lot of different political subjects, none of them making any sense to me, but I remember particularly an old professor who had created his own subject at the university, which he called "An Introduction to Civic Education." There was no textbook for his course, and we had four straight hours with him every Monday during my first semester. He spoke not one sentence that made any sense, but we had to take notes on his every word. There wasn't anything frightening in his words, but everyone knew how dangerous this man could be. You just could sense it.

One Monday morning while I was taking my notes, I got hungry and took out my sandwich from the bag and started eating.

"What are you doing there?" the professor asked sharply.

"Sorry—I got really hungry," I fearfully replied.

"What is your name?" he continued. I gave him the information he needed, and he continued, "Do you know that I could dismiss you from my course for the thing you have done today?"

"I am really sorry, sir, Mr. Professor," I answered.

"I am not 'sir' but a comrade professor," he said angrily. "Sit down! Don't try anything else stupid like this!" Everybody looked at me and after the class a number of students came to me and warned me, "It could be a really serious mistake for you and for your future here." From that time on, I started to do my best and tried to go unnoticed in his class, hoping he would forget about my incident.

The date of the exam came, and I was prepared as well as I could be.

"Show me your notes from the class," he said at the beginning of the oral exam. I wasn't sure if he remembered my name and face from the large class of one hundred students. I knew he liked colors and underlining, so I had carefully marked passages throughout my notes.

"That's good!" He looked visibly satisfied and started asking me a lot of questions. I did so well on his examination that he wrote "excellent," which is the best grade you can receive at the university. But after he wrote the grade in my exam book, he looked in the roll book to check on my attendance in his class. Suddenly, his face turned red. "What did you do in my class?" he asked.

"I was eating in your class one day," I said almost hopelessly.

"Well, I don't remember, but it's really stupid of you," he said.

"I know. Sorry."

"It could harm your grade, do you know that?" he asked me.

"I know."

"You did so well today. Do you know that you are the only one so far who has gotten a grade of 'excellent'?" He looked at me as I stood there silent. Finally he was ready to pronounce a verdict: "Go, you silly. I have already written the grade, and you are just lucky today." I left his office as soon as possible to make sure that he wouldn't change his mind.

On the way home I wondered what had made him so compassionate in the end that he didn't change his mind about my grade. I came to only one thought: He had a really old picture on the wall in his office, of Lenin sitting with two children, a boy and a girl, caressing their hair. I remembered that before the professor wrote down my grade in my exam book, he asked me, "What do you think this picture represents?" I was surprised by his question, but I looked at the picture and replied after a few seconds of pondering, "All the teachers and parents in the world should show more love and hope to their students and children for the better future of all humans." For a small moment there was a silence, and I noticed that he was somehow moved by my response. He replied, "I haven't heard a student tell me anything like this . . ."

He was an old man, a strong Communist. I learned later that everybody was afraid of him, even other Communists at the university. He was pretty much left alone, soaked up in his own civic education philosophy and without any colleagues or friends.

It was a test of human endurance to sit in the Marxist-Leninist philosophy class. There was a spirit of mental bondage and prison there. At least in a prison cell a person could scream, but at the university you couldn't. A class could be so impossibly boring that you just had to hold your head in both hands to survive and not sleep. The next class would be so tense and irritating, from all the lies presented to you, that you would have a huge headache afterwards.

The Communist professors fed us with the idea of defeating capitalism by a process of fighting against it and hating it, thus achieving an ideal Communist society, where everybody would be equal, loving, and compassionate to each other. It didn't make any sense, not even to those who didn't know anything about God. While I was talking to some students, I found out that they didn't actually have any desire to live in a "Communist dream society" like that, because it would mean a change of their behavior and manners completely to the opposite of what they were presently living. They spoke very cynically and ironically about the future in a Communist society. In those classes I felt as if professors presented an impossible high bar and expected students to jump over it. Or, to put it another way, the professors were like barking dogs in the middle of the night with a full moon: they had to bark, but they didn't know exactly why nor for how long.

There were a few different categories of Communist professors. One was a group of people who were fanatically committed to the philosophy. They were devoted as if they were the best missionaries of Communism. They would sacrifice everything—their families, personal life, their time at work and outside of work. I called them Communist-aholics. Many of these were bachelors or single women. However, even inside this group there were variations. A few of them weren't dangerous, but rather naive to their subject of study. Students would take advantage of this type of professor, asking some careful questions that would throw doubt on the Communist system. This kind of class was almost like comical theater: a student with a "trick" question had to be extremely careful toward classmates, in order to avoid alarming any secret police student sitting and watching the process, but on the other hand the student's question could be clever enough that the answer could give a funny message to the rest of the class. The professor would be discussing and defending his Communist ideas from the textbook so faithfully and repeatedly that after a while everyone in the class would know that the whole thing was pure buffoonery. Other professors committed to Communism were very dangerous and could get a student in deep trouble if he or she would even try to question any Marxist-Leninist ideas.

Then there was a group of professors with a great amount of power at the university because of their membership in the Communist party. They may or may not be intelligent. You could find among them many varieties of people—drinkers, snobs, frivolous types, and extremely dangerous people. This group knew that the whole Communist idea was absolute nonsense. But that was also their strongest weapon. Their word could be an ultimate end to your career at the university. These people were committed to only one thing—their own corruption. They would take money, cars, and other material privileges in exchange for admitting students who were sons and daughters of Communists but who didn't have good enough grades to make it into the university and were admitted only because of the high price their parents would pay to these corrupted Communists. Of course, the Communists were very smart, and you could read in the newspapers occasionally that some leading Communist person was kicked out of the university or a high post in society because of corruption. It was again only arranged theater. Everything was arranged far in advance—to get rid of even some Communists who became a problem to the government when they got a little bit too prosperous and therefore overstepped certain Communist-allowed barriers.

Everyone could feel the fearful, repressive and vexing spirit which was poured out from the Marxist-Leninist philosophy statements. There wasn't place for any real discussion about even one possible doubt that there could be something wrong with the philosophy, because everything was presented by the professors as being perfectly clear, with the Communist regime headed toward a great future and the final, total destruction of capitalism. The professors were certain about the future victory of Communism on our planet. They were real ideological fanatics, very serious about life, and if you tried to discuss anything with them, they turned it into an absolute roller coaster of nonsense, often going on at such length that I suspected them of not knowing where the truth was or what the original question was. They were the best and most advanced lying rhetoricians I have ever seen in my life, using a lot of ear-splitting words, with passionate and hungry power in the melody of the voice, coupled with the most logical, precise skill of using the right words in the right order at the right time.

The majority of the professors teaching these Marxist-Leninist classes were members of the Communist party, or those who were potential candidates to become so. Already a couple of my fellow students were members of the Communist party. When I found out about them, it was a very scary feeling to know that someone as young as me was already an official Communist. I couldn't comprehend what kind of young person would make such a decision. Later on, I realized, with the rest of our study group, that one of them was studying with us but actually working for the secret police. He was like a squirrel running and jumping around us everywhere, wanting to know our opinions on recent politics, the president, the government, Russia, America, Western Europe, etc. It took us a couple of years to find him out because he was very smart in his strategy to get close to everyone and was very skilled at creating just the right atmosphere, wherein we would say what was really on our mind. He was a friendly but dangerous fellow. Fortunately, as we matured we became more careful around him.

I particularly remember one Communist professor who was always uncompromising toward her students. She was an older lady whose husband was one of the deans at the university. They didn't have any children and both were devoted only to their work. She could be very hard to get along with. I had a chance to see her after my studies at the university and was surprised how differently she talked to me when I wasn't her student anymore. She became somewhat more friendly, and we kept in touch for several years; however, she was disappointed in me later when I talked to her about my belief in God. After the revolution in 1989, they both hid like mice in their apartment and didn't want to make contact with anyone. That might have been a good idea; although they both were retired from teaching by the time of the Velvet Revolution, they had lost the respect of the university students due to the couple's adamant Communist attitude. In January 1995, her husband sent me a small card saying that both were seriously ill. He wrote, "A great catastrophe has met both of us. My wife has been paralyzed on half of her body, and cannot speak and communicate, and I am dying of a cancer." A few months later I learned that he had died. I wrote his wife a letter but never got a response from her, though I eventually learned that she was in a nursing home in Brno. I have given a lot of thought to their situation. What a sad end it must have been for both of them, who had tasted real power to destroy many of their students' careers, to then end up without any family or friends, left just to themselves, their illnesses, and their disbelief in God. That would be a very bitter and hopeless ending to one's life story.

One of the subjects in physical education in my first semester was human anatomy. During one class the professor was teaching about sport physical therapy, and he spoke highly of the great effects of yoga on muscles and the nervous system generally. I was very interested in yoga as a type of relaxation. After the class, I asked him for the address of a yoga club in the city. I decided to go to check out this idea.

I was amazed at how flexible the fifty-year-old yoga teacher was. The class was unbelievably quiet, and everybody seemed to be very concentrated, having refocused from the outside to the inside world. It was very new to me. I started taking the class and searched in my university library for more about yoga.

One of my fellow students, while traveling back to school one weekend, met a man on the train who spoke to her about yoga. She gave me his address and told me that we could visit him together if I was interested. We went to his place together, and I met Mr. Otakar Vojkůvka, a man who seemed to be in his sixties or seventies. I assumed that he was interested only in yoga, and yet, I was surprised by how much this man knew about life in general.

When we walked into his living room, we saw a small, round coffee table, and on the table's surface was a picture of pioneers crossing the plains en route to Utah. Looking at the picture, I sensed the pioneers' hard work, perseverance, patience, and focus on something really important.

"What's that?" I asked Mr. Vojkůvka.

"The first pioneers traveling to Utah," he said.

I didn't understand it, but I felt it was probably a part of the great American history I had never learned at school. Therefore, I was ashamed and too embarrassed to ask further questions that day. Though I didn't know anything about his religious affiliation at that time, I mark that brief visit as one of the most important events of my life: Mr. Vojkůvka (I would later learn) was the very first Czech Latter-day Saint I had ever met. I was twenty years old. When my friend and I left his house, I felt something sweet and beautiful in my heart that I could hardly express even to my friend, who was talking to me about it. I didn't know what it was exactly that I felt, but I knew I had to go back to that house.

It was so different going to the Marxist-Leninist class directly after this visit. The atmosphere in the classroom seemed to be from a strange world in comparison to the sweet spirit in the house I had just visited an hour or so ago.

We arranged another meeting with him, but next time my friend couldn't go with me. During this second visit I had a chance to see Mr. Vojkůvka's son, Gád, his daughter-in-law, Magda, and their children Gád Junior and Miriam. I was warmly welcomed by Mr. Vojkůvka. We sat down, and his son Gád also joined us this time. We chatted a little bit, and Gád asked me a question.

"So you are interested in yoga?"

"I don't know anything about yoga, but I would like to learn because you all seem to be so happy. I assume it's because of yoga."

I didn't have a chance to continue the discussion with Mr. Vojkůvka's son Gád that day because Gád's wife needed a hand in the garden, but I continued talking with the older Mr. Vojkůvka.

"So you would like to learn how to be happy?" Mr. Vojkůvka started.

"Well, Mr. Vojkůvka, there is something really special about the atmosphere of your home that I haven't experienced before."

"What is that?" he asked.

"I cannot describe it, but I had to really think about the unique spirit I felt from my last visit in your home." I looked around his room, where there were at least three large bookcases filled with books I hadn't seen before. "I have never seen book covers like these. What are they?" I asked.

"Most of them are different translations of ancient scriptures and writings," he said plainly.

"Did you translate all of them?"

"Mostly my wife did. Since she passed away I haven't had any new translations."

"Well, your hobby must be studying all of these books."

"More than a hobby."

"What is it?"

"It's my whole life. Without studying good literature you cannot grow spiritually at all."

I was wondering what this spirituality could be that this man was talking about. Was it some kind of magic? He interrupted my short pondering. "Many people don't even know why they live and what is the purpose of their life."

"Frankly, Mr. Vojkůvka, do you think that there is a certain purpose of life? Isn't it foolish to try to figure out an answer to the question which was asked by many philosophers from ancient times and which has been answered so many different and confusing ways?"

"I think it's crucial to our lives. Without answering this question, we are lost in the middle of the universe and life doesn't mean anything. It's like a boat shaking on the sea. No direction. No real happiness." He looked straight into my eyes.

"Do you think that to know the purpose of human life actually brings happiness?" I asked.

"Well, if you find real truth, then you have a key to happiness."

"But how can you find pure truth? What is it? Which philosophy owns it?"

"None. None of them," he answered and continued, "There is more than philosophy."

His daughter-in-law knocked on his door, indicating that it was time for dinner.

"I am sorry. I guess we'll have to continue another time," he said.

"That's all right; I understand."

"Well, before you leave, I'll give you this small book. Read it and tell me what you think about it." The book was from Sri Swami Sivananda, an Indian yogi—that is, an individual who practices yoga—and it was titled *Searching for Happiness with God.*

What a strange title, I thought, but I took it. As I left Mr. Vojkůvka's house, I marveled at the fact that someone had actually asked me a serious question about my life and its meaning—and had asked in a very different way than I was used to hearing from Communists, school, newspapers, and even my church. He was serious and didn't laugh, and he wasn't cynical or sarcastic as my school or university teachers or my schoolmates were when asked similar questions. With most people I knew, a question about the meaning of life was not even taken seriously—just answered hastily and on the surface. Even in my church I didn't hear discussions about the true meaning of life. Rather I saw that all of the members were followers, some more faithful than others, probably never asking life's questions with the sincere depth that I had heard from this man I had just met. I was sitting in the park that afternoon and suddenly felt that there was something very significant happening in my life. I didn't know what it was, but I knew that since that discussion my thoughts and attitude about life had seemed different.

I opened the book he gave to me, and after a few lines I realized that although I had not thought about my beliefs or labeled myself, I was a longtime atheist—a victim and product of the Communist school system I had grown up with. I realized that whatever my faith was, it was somehow affected by all the thoughts that came to me from school. "Ten thousand times repeated, a lie becomes true" was my life's reality. It was hard to admit it, but it was bitterly true. I found that I was against anything that smelled of Communist ideology, but I also suddenly saw that my own life was focused only on fighting against the wall of the current ideology I lived in, and I had not found my own proactive direction. I realized I had forgotten about my private, personal well-being while fighting. I hadn't made any time and effort except to fight against the dragon. Later I realized that one of Satan's powerful tools is to surround a person with something so obviously negative that the person spends all his or her energy only on nonsensical fighting, instead of turning their backs to it and trying to find their own pace and direction. How much time did I waste only on pointing to the wrong side of the world, instead of hiking towards a better future? Somehow this big beast of Communism had become the focus of my personal life, as it had for many of my fellowmen, and meanwhile I experienced a complete emptiness as I considered my human soul and its place in the world and in the universe. I didn't know who I was, where I came from, or what the purpose of my life was.

If nothing else, the visit left these ponderings in my heart. I felt happy because it was clear to me that I had found someone whom I could trust, who wouldn't laugh at my questions and who would listen to me. Someone who was really into life.

CHAPTER

6

FINDING SOME ANSWERS

I went back a few weeks later to visit the older gentleman, Mr. Vojkůvka, but he was out of town. Then the exam period came, and I was very busy taking tests. After three months or so, I decided to visit Mr. Vojkůvka again.

"Oh, I thought you had completely forgotten about me," he said when he saw me standing at his front door.

"Well, I have some questions for you," I began.

"I thought so," he said, smiling and inviting me in.

"I don't understand what sense it makes to be a real believer in God. The book you have given to me speaks all about it," I continued.

"Do you have any specific question?" he said, raising his eyebrows.

"Actually, I do—a lot," I answered a little bit hesitantly.

"Well, let's start," he replied, and I felt that suddenly our visit changed into a small religious conference.

I learned very new things for me—that to believe in God is to experience real happiness and joy. I found myself smiling, although I had a lot of doubtful questions, such as How can you know this when you haven't seen God? But even as I questioned,

simultaneously I felt really comfortable and experienced the very
first real discussion about God in my life. It was so new to me to
see someone openly, freely, and happily talking about God. He was
sure about his responses to my questions. I found myself wondering, while he was answering my questions, How is it possible that
he is so sure and that what he says sounds so real? I felt that this
man had knowledge about life and its meaning which all of my
professors at the university couldn't even possibly dream of,
though he had not earned any university degree.

After this visit, I asked him a question, which surprised even
myself: "Can you be my teacher for a while and help me learn
about God?"

"Well, certainly I can help you," he responded.

"What's my homework for the next conference?" I asked, and
saw his little smile.

"For the next time, you just write your own journal every day,"
he answered. That sounds a little bit off the subject of God, I
thought, but I respected his suggestion.

"What should I write down every day?" I asked.

"Your thoughts about the things we talked about, and especially your new questions which will come up while studying the
book."

I left his home and can remember as if it were yesterday that
as I did so, I felt like a completely new person. New and real—
because I had never heard what I had heard that day. My soul experienced a measure of happiness which I had not ever discovered
before. Taking a tram in Brno, I held the handle and felt the tremendous energy of joy pumping into my heart and soul. I feel happy,
really happy as never before, I pondered, and felt like a witness
who was just observing someone else's life. Is it real? I wondered
while coming back to one of the philosophical classes at the university that day. Yes, it is real. The feeling of fullness from the discussion remained in my heart even through the boring philosophy

lesson that day. My mind was engaged in intense thinking and pondering, but also in peaceful happiness. There wasn't the same doubt which I felt so deeply and bitterly just the day before I visited this Latter-day Saint brother. I wrote my first spiritual thoughts and reactions in my journal during this Marxist-Leninist philosophy class. It felt so new, so wonderful, to write the thoughts from my own heart. I even smiled at my Communist professor in the class. He returned the smile to me and I thought, Well, you would be surprised and not happy if you knew my thoughts and realized why I am smiling at you. I am sure we both had completely opposite reasons to smile that day.

Suddenly, God became the topic of new exploration of my life. My life began to change even before I knew and could comprehend for sure that God was real and that he cared for me personally. I couldn't understand at the beginning of my spiritual path that God had a body, that Jesus Christ could offer a sacrifice for every man. Yet I did experience a total change of self after these two visits with a Latter-day Saint, and I still didn't even know he was a member. I couldn't understand the gospel at that point, and probably if I had been at that time sitting in an LDS chapel, I would have been totally lost. It would have been very strong spiritual meat to digest. However, I do believe that I experienced this personal change for two reasons. First, I had met a Latter-day Saint who had a strong testimony of God, and I felt the spirit of the testimony; and second, I was tremendously spiritually hungry, starving for this new spiritual feast that had come into my life. I knew that I had been looking for this for a long time.

This is it—my real life is beginning, I thought when I walked out of the door of Mr. Vojkůvka's after my second visit.

Starting with the second visit with the elderly Mr. Vojkůvka, I did feel a much deeper distance between me and other schoolmates and even the professors. This distance at school was sensed mainly as I felt in their presence a tired, gloomy, and confused spirit, a closed umbrella: it was not possible to be really sincere, sharing, and open with them anymore. I missed that as I contrasted this dark feeling with the open, unbridled spirit of the Latter-day Saints, although at the time, of course, I didn't even realize that they belonged to a church. The spirit of openness and family together-ness was amazing—so new to me, so wonderful and relieving.

It was a shock to find myself even more alone because of my very new spiritual discoveries, but nevertheless, I knew from my heart that I was doing the right thing and that this loneliness was just a part of my growing—to struggle with the outside physical and Communist world.

I wasn't the kind of Christian who could be loving and caring to others right from the beginning. I actually felt the opposite in the beginning of my spiritual path—I felt further from others. When I look back today, I understand that the negative feeling was a part of the Communist sickness I grew up with. Everybody had a secret. For their own purposes, the Communists encouraged people to close doors to each other and thus to fear their neighbors and keep their distance from each other. Nobody would share his or her deep thoughts in public. We didn't discuss life's serious matters. My Czech countrymen would keep silent—mainly because of fear of bringing troubles to themselves or their families.

While I was reading Sivananda's book, I came across the sub-ject of prayer and meditation. From my Protestant religious back-ground I had known and heard only one prayer, and that was the Lord's Prayer. I had never thought that any other kind of prayer existed. And meditation was something so far from my compre-hension that I always thought of it as a thing of Far Eastern origin and therefore as something that couldn't be of any help for a European soul. However, while I was reading, I realized that both prayer and meditation are so essential to our lives that without them no personal progress and happiness could be possible. Above all, I learned that a prayer is also a vital key in communication with God.

Wow! That was a little bit too much—We can actually communicate with God? It appeared to me so grandiose and extravagant on one side, and so revealing—like watching the first astronaut walk on the moon.

How, I pondered, can we communicate with God? Has anyone actually ever communicated with him in the twentieth century? How would it feel? What would it mean to have an experience like that? Is it possible, or is it just a lifetime goal of every Christian and yogi? I thought about these questions and was totally immersed in the book. I learned through my reading that to become a good person means to gradually get rid of all bad habits, to clean the mind and body on an everyday basis. The book suggested that it is necessary to exercise yoga asanas (postures) every day, because they help to establish the correct positive attitude toward one's body and mind. The exercises would help a person to overcome well-known human weaknesses such as laziness, selfishness, poor eating habits, building and softening a human soul to see everyday life challenges as unique and unforgettable opportunities. It seemed to be unbelievable that physical exercise could do so much! I also read that actually yoga isn't for everyone because it requires a lot of effort and that a lot of students stop in the middle of their way and lose their progress. According to the author, who was of course a non-Christian, this is why people have to be born again and try over and over until they succeed in that cleansing process.

"I don't like the idea," I said when I sat down and visited Mr. Vojkůvka next time. "Do you believe in reincarnation?"

"Not at all," he answered.

"Well, are you a Christian or a yogi?" I asked.

"I accept some ideas from yoga, but I am a Christian."

"Why do you think that yoga could be any good for a Christian? A Christian's outlook is in conflict with the idea of reincarnation, don't you think?" I asked.

"I don't think yoga can provide answers for a Christian, but it can be an excellent way for an atheist in this country to become eventually a Christian," he replied.

"How did you come to this idea?" I continued.

"Because I have seen a lot of people in this country become so while following this path," he said. Then he added, "it is very hard for a person living in this country to come to a true understanding of God's nature, don't you think? They know nothing about him. Yoga is a detour that works to bring many atheists to the path of truth. Yoga softens an atheist's mind. And that's the very first step."

He then told me of his introduction to yoga: "Many years ago, when I and my wife, Tessy, found ourselves in a situation in which we couldn't practice our religion and were persecuted for our faith, we still felt that we wanted to progress spiritually. We were invited by one old professor in Brno to dinner, and while sitting in his living room, he offered us a look at the books he had there. My wife opened an English book, which she started reading, and I could just see that her attention was completely centered on the book's contents.

"She started to read me a couple of pages from one of the yogis in India. We both were so interested in the book that the professor gave it to us. And that was the beginning of yoga in the Vojkůvka family." He told me of his communication by letter with Mr. Sivananda, and that led to a further mention of his family's persecution because of religious beliefs—though he didn't specify any particular religion as he talked. "The secret police were watching and spying on us. Occasionally, we were lucky and got a Christmas card from our U.S. friends, but it happened rarely. We were completely cut off from the outside world and were questioned by police many times."

"How long have you experienced this persecution?" I asked, listening to him almost without breathing.

"It has been almost forty years. It got a little bit better after I got older and my wife passed away."

I knew this man was telling me the truth. He mentioned that he had even served a brief prison term because of his beliefs. It made me think highly of his life and his family. I didn't yet know anything about his membership in the Church, but I thought, What a man, who has kept searching for a better life and happiness in this country and has gone through so many persecutions.

I started to attend a small class which Mr. Vojkůvka offered me and which was held in his home. We were only three students—a fire eater/sword swallower at the circus, a man just diagnosed with cancer, and I. An interesting combination! We met once in the middle of the week to discuss various topics about life. Mr. Vojkůvka mainly focused on maintaining a positive attitude toward oneself and explained to us why it was so essential to our lives. I kept my journal and started doing regular yoga exercises, even concentration and meditation. The man from the circus traveled a lot and didn't come regularly. The other man was really depressed by his health situation, and Mr. Vojkůvka would spend the whole hour talking to him about a positive attitude and how important it could be for his healing. I learned so much just by listening and watching this older man who was trying to get better any way he could! After a few weeks he stopped coming for some time, and I remained as the last attending member of the class.

As we continued our discussions, I felt that my life was becoming different. Although Brother Vojkůvka was very careful not to name any specific church, his discussions focused more and more on Christ's life. During this period, I tasted many times a warm and reassuring feeling in my heart that the things I was learning were right. I hadn't experienced anything like that before as I had carefully studied many philosophers and their ideas. Yes, there was often an excitement for a newly discovered knowledge, but to listen to Mr. Vojkůvka brought me happiness which came from the brain, heart, and soul together. As almost an irreligious person with a pint-sized knowledge about God and Christ, I was blessed and touched by the Holy Ghost, and I felt two clear and distinct new lines in my heart: first, joy, and second, a desire to learn about the meaning of life.

I reflected on my life to that point, and it seemed as if the years before I had met Mr. Vojkůvka and learned these truths had not even been real life. It was as if I had not begun my life until this point when I had started really to be happy and had at last found a true teacher, one who knew the answers to life's great questions. It wasn't that I had not been trying to figure life out before, but because of the society and Marxist-Leninist philosophy at school, it became a very discouraging topic, complete with confusions and irony. Above all, I had never heard in my church a real conversation on the meaning of human life.

I had a lot of intellectual difficulties in the beginning as I tried to understand who God is and that he has a body and isn't just a great universal power without any form. There were no roots in my heart and soul to accept naturally and without an intellectual fight the idea that God has a body. The main mistake in my spiritual beginnings was that I was trying to understand God only through studying about him and trying to obtain more knowledge about his work. I thought this was the way to understand him. The missing part—pondering and finding him through my heart—was eventually quite a discovery for me. However, God was so good to me in my embryonic spiritual stage. He knew better, and I was able to feel his love and to see him even with my spiritual eyes partially closed and despite my lack of understanding.

All these new spiritual discoveries led me to a new desire to give real direction to my life. Suddenly, I understood that finding God wasn't embracing him on a philosophical and intellectual level but rather in a very simple down-to-earth way—doing something with my own life, making a commitment and following through. A new spiritual understanding led me to think more and more about what I was going to do with this incredible gift of life that was given to me. I felt prompted to make a serious start.

The yoga activities were all right, but I missed in yoga a personal commitment to God that would help me to be a real, orderly, and valid part of his organized work during my time on the earth. I didn't feel comfortable having my spiritual life just as my new hobby—some kind of a secret which would bring a smile to my face and flexibility to my joints and skeleton, or just as an intellectual, inner superiority or protection from the bad world around me. It wasn't so much a criticism of yoga; it was just a way I came to understand my life. I do respect a lot of great yogis for their moral example to others. Above all, I have a lot of great, wonderful yogi friends who live exemplary lives, and I respect them and will always cherish my association with them.

Every new spiritual understanding of God's laws opened my eyes and my heart. I was learning bit by bit. Until this point I still had not heard one word about the Church. One day during our usual discussion, I expressed my feelings to Mr. Vojkůvka. I told him, "I feel that I want to start my new life with some kind of a new start and a new belonging. It probably sounds strange to you, and maybe it isn't possible. But I am having a hard time dealing with the two worlds around me. First, the Communist one, which I don't favor, but nevertheless I am required to live in it. The second, this new, amazing spiritual life which I have found in taking your small seminars. I would love to be entirely part of some kind of a spiritual world with firm laws and directions. If life here can be so horrible for so many people who have to suffer because of Communism and its devious philosophy, there must be a living truth on the other side, which is organized as well, don't you think? If it does not exist now, it might perhaps exist in the future—I hope. There has to be something that stands in opposition to all the lies— something strong enough to face up and fight for a better world. What do you think?"

Mr. Vojkůvka was evidently surprised by my conflicts. First, he didn't say anything, and then he walked to one of his bookcases and looked for a book.

"Here it is. Could you help me reach it in the upper shelf there?" he asked.

"Sure," I replied, and pulled off the upper shelf a book written on a typewriter.

"I think you will enjoy it," he said, "and it can answer a question you have asked today."

I opened the copy immediately and read *A Skeptic Discovers Mormonism,* by Timberline Wales Riggs. It didn't ring any bell; how could it? I liked the word *discovers* in the title. "How long can I have it?" I asked.

"Until you finish it" was his short answer.

This book was the very first work from which I learned about The Church of Jesus Christ of Latter-day Saints. I came to my dormitory late that evening and started reading. I read the entire book overnight. Each page was like a new hope, like a question posed and then answered immediately with the full acceptance of my heart, all while reading the book. I loved all the ideas and teachings, but I had a great aversion to any kind of church. At that time, I thought any church represented just another organization designed to gain power over the people. For that reason, I didn't want to depend on any organization or church, and I thought, Well, this Mormonism is great; I just wish it wasn't a church. I repeated this thought the next day while visiting the Vojkůvka family.

"That's fine. I understand your concern. I will give you another book which speaks a little bit more about the organization of the Latter-day Saints, so that you can see some differences and can compare this with the attitude and knowledge you have about churches so far."

He gave me a book titled *Priesthood and Church Government*

in The Church of Jesus Christ of Latter-day Saints by John A. Widtsoe. I read the book and came back again.

"I am fascinated by the happy life attitude of these people," I said to Mr. Vojkůvka. "It's such a shame that they are only in America. We will probably never know as much as we would like about them. With the ideas they have, they must live fascinating lives, don't you think?"

"Well, they are in the United States, but there are a few of them in our country also," he said.

"Have you ever met any of them?" I asked with hope.

"Yes, actually I have met and know a lot of them."

"Could you give me the address of a Czech Mormon?"

"You don't need any address. You are in the home of one of them."

I could hardly comprehend what he was saying at that moment. My first thought was, I haven't seen anyone else living in this house except for the Vojkůvka family. Then suddenly it hit me, and I knew that I was sitting in the house with a Latter-day Saint.

"Yes, I am a Mormon. I am a Latter-day Saint," he said, answering my unspoken question.

"Is it possible to be a Saint?" I asked, thinking in old terms of the Catholic church's stone monuments to all the different saints, always depicted with haloes above their heads. I was particularly thinking in that moment about the statues at the famous Charles Bridge in Prague. Mr. Vojkůvka didn't look like any of them.

"Yes and no," he answered.

"I thought that all the applicants for sainthood have to be dead first," I told him. He laughed when he heard me.

"They need to work on sainthood during their lifetime," he said.

"They must have a very hard life then," I continued.

"Why do you think so?"

"Because to be a saint surely requires a lot of prayers and spiritual activities."

"Not only that," he said, "but they also have to be good fathers, mothers, neighbors, workers, doctors, teachers, citizens, etc. Their life has to shine for the rest of their countrymen, wherever they live. Their actions should show truth and integrity—their excellent work and positive life attitude, no matter what kind of circumstances they are living in. The truth of the gospel should shine through their everyday happiness and joy. To be pure in heart—this is what it means to be a saint."

"It's fascinating, but it sounds like a dream."

"Well, Olga, the reality is that this very moment while we are sitting here, there are millions of members, young and old, who are striving to live this high standard and rise above their daily struggles, and many of them are capable of doing so. And do you know why they can do it? Because their teaching is pure truth, not a half, a quarter, or a little bit, or almost the whole truth. Their teaching has a fulness of the truth."

I will never forget this sentence because it became an essential turning point toward this religion. If there was anything in my life I wanted to know, it was pure truth. I thought that it didn't exist because it seemed to be beyond the comprehension of any human, from all the school and other public discussion I had heard so far in my life. But here I heard that it existed! And that actually there are people who live the law of pure truth! It was amazing. Somehow I reached toward the idea, at that moment, that with pure and full truth must come the end of the emotional, physical, or any kind of bondage a person has endured.

"I thought that I could not be more happy than I am already, but now I can see that there is a new world ahead of me to grasp and discover. I want to be happy in truth, because I haven't been happy in all the lies I have had to hear at school all my life."

"I understand you very well," he said, "but you have to keep both feet on the ground, so to speak, and finish your education, which will bring you more freedom to choose your future life." I could clearly see that he was answering my unspoken question: What sense does it make to continue at a university that teaches me lies from morning until evening?

"Everything has to have a purpose. Sometimes we don't have a choice because of the society we are living in now. Do you know the proverb 'Člověk, který sedí na vrbě je hlupák, když si nevyřeže píšťaličku' ('It would be silly for a man who is sitting in a willow tree not to carve a whistle')? What it means is that sometimes you can use the very same weapon of your enemy to actually win him over."

"I don't know what you mean," I said.

"Even the nonsense Marxist-Leninist philosophy you have to study, plus all other ancient and modern philosophies that are great but somehow still a half-truth and also twisted by Communists, could be a great tool to know in the future as you learn what to say and how to explain real truth. You can help a lot of people this way."

The idea of helping others sounded unbelievable in my country's corrupted society, but I accepted the strong spirit of truthfulness in the words of this seventy-year-old man. His words were to me like a shining torch, and I listened to his firm testimony about my life's possibilities. You can imagine how I felt at that moment. I thought it was not possible to open another door in my life, and to my surprise, I find even the hope to live a meaningful life and actually help others. Nobody had ever talked to me like that in my life—not even my parents, who loved me dearly. If they could have, they would have done so, but since they did not yet know about the true church, there wasn't such a possibility. I felt as if the candle of my real life was lit that evening. I asked for a copy of the Book of Mormon, which I had noticed was quoted many times in *A Skeptic Discovers Mormonism*.

I came to the dormitory. My roommate wasn't at home that night, and I was free to open the first pages and start to read the Book of Mormon. It was very hard in the beginning, and I almost fell asleep—I couldn't find any relevant connection in the history of these people who left Jerusalem. I made a lot of notes with the questions I needed to ask. But when I came to 2 Nephi 2:25, I read the words "Adam fell that men might be; and men are, that they might have joy." I sat completely motionless, unable to even move, such was the way this truth entered my soul at that moment. It shocked me with an enormous amount of happiness which suddenly opened my heart, and I had not experienced anything like that before. I kept reading this sentence over and over and over, always filled with an embracing new happiness in my heart and a new understanding as I did so. I was deeply moved. Here in this book I had at last found an answer to my long-held question, and somehow, deep in my soul, I believed the statement that the purpose of human life was to have joy! But I would never have thought that I myself, without anyone sitting with me in the room, might find the answer to my question about the purpose of life, nor could I have imagined that such a strong, unshakable assurance of the Spirit would come to my soul from reading the words.

It was around midnight that I experienced a strong spiritual witness, a feeling of great joy in every cell of my body because of the new ideas that had entered my soul and given me new life. My heart was filled with a love and joy which I never knew before, and my mind was perfectly clear, with no doubtful thought or feeling. Suddenly, one single, pure thought came to my lips: "God lives!" I listened to my own words and felt the reality of God in my life as his love filled my whole being. I knelt down for the first time in prayer, expressing silently my gratitude and love for the life he had given to me. I felt how much he loved me, and that in the same way, he loved every living soul on this earth.

I would later review again and again this experience, and my thoughts would fill me with the certainty of God's existence, which has become since that day a real part of myself, without any doubt.

I knew that something very significant had happened in my life that night, which wouldn't be understood if shared with any professor at the university nor with my schoolmates nor even with my own family members. From that moment, my perspective was changed. I felt a tremendous joy and desire to become good in a new way after this very first spiritual experience in my life. I felt an urgency to finish something old inside of me and to make a new beginning. Although it sounded strange, it felt real. I didn't understand what kind of change had to occur in my life, but I felt for the first time that belonging to something good and pure, guided by God's true rules and truth, was possible in this life and on this earth.

What is it and where is it? I wondered. I could hardly wait to go and visit Mr. Vojkůvka early the next morning, and I had no doubt he would help me. I felt a happy urgency to act that morning.

"What happened?" he asked me when I rang the bell around eight in the morning.

"I have to talk to you," I said. After I had shared the night's experience, I told him that ever since then, I had felt an urgent need to change in my heart. "Is there any way I can start my life like a new person?" I asked.

"Yes, there is."

"What is that?"

"I'll show you in the scriptures." He opened his Bible, and we read John 3:5: "Except a man be born of water and of the Spirit, he cannot enter into the kingdom of God."

At first I didn't understand that these words of Jesus referred to the need for the baptism. I asked, "What does it mean to enter the kingdom of God?"

"To become his disciple, be baptized, and keep all God's

commandments, work on our eternal progression and our personal perfection, and to bring more souls to God's kingdom," he answered me.

"I was already baptized as a newborn baby. Does it count?" I asked.

"No, it doesn't count. Let me read you a scripture about it." He opened the Book of Mormon and read from Moroni 8:11–15:

> And their little children need no repentance, neither baptism. Behold, baptism is unto repentance to the fulfilling the commandments unto the remission of sins.
>
> But little children are alive in Christ, even from the foundation of the world; if not so, God is a partial God, and also a changeable God, and a respecter to persons; for how many little children have died without baptism!
>
> Wherefore, if little children could not be saved without baptism, these must have gone to an endless hell.
>
> Behold I say unto you, that he that supposeth that little children need baptism is in the gall of bitterness and in the bonds of iniquity; for he hath neither faith, hope, nor charity; wherefore, should he be cut off while in the thought, he must go down to hell.
>
> For awful is the wickedness to suppose that God saveth one child because of baptism, and the other must perish because he hath no baptism.

"Wow! It means that my baptism doesn't count, my parents' baptisms don't count, and the baptisms of many others I know don't count either, because most of them were baptized as newborn babies. That's great news, because I don't even remember that event, anyway." This was really starting to roll!

"Baptism is a step we must take to enter the Lord's kingdom on earth, and through baptism we become members of his church, which has been organized to help the people to work on their eternal progress," he said.

While he was saying these words, my heart was filled with great joy, and I came to a sudden understanding that this desire of belonging had actually been in my heart since childhood. However, I hadn't understood that specific feeling ever before in the way I could comprehend at that moment. Now I recognized that what I had always dreamed of was to be actually a part of the Lord's kingdom. Many times in my youth there were moments of loneliness, and I questioned the world and wondered if there really was any pure living society of really good people I could look up to and take their great lives as examples and strength so that I could make it and be a good person myself. Most of these times I thought, "Well, all those people who are great are alone or dead." To be a good person in the Communist society in which I grew up amounted to being stupid, although in all their textbooks we of course read just the opposite. The word *good* was always connected in real life with the hidden Communist synonym *silly* or even *not intelligent enough.*

"What do I have to do in order to be baptized?" I asked.

"There are six lessons you have to learn before you get baptized," he answered.

"Can I get them and learn them so that I could pass an exam as soon as possible and be baptized?"

"Well, these lessons are a little bit different from the ones you usually take at school," he responded with a little smile on his face. He invited me to come next Sunday to his house, where there would be a gathering of members of The Church of Jesus Christ of Latter-day Saints. I couldn't wait. I didn't know what to expect exactly, but felt very privileged that I could come to a such a meeting.

I was surprised. When I came to the meeting, I saw a handful of very old grandmas and grandpas in addition to the Vojkůvka family. I couldn't believe my eyes. I thought, Is this church meant for old people only? I was shocked when I saw all the old men

wearing their suits and ties—it reminded me of Communist meetings, because normally people would wear suits with ties only for
weddings, funerals, or special celebrations. A suit for an occasion
other than these was a sign of a Communist or a foreigner from the
West. These old men spoke Czech. I calmed down when I saw all
the women wearing neat dresses. "Yes, it must be a special occasion," I reassured myself. I was the only one dressed casually that
Sunday. Soon Mr. Vojkůvka introduced me to all these members,
and among them were a couple of middle-aged men. I understood
from the place they were sitting during the meeting later on that
they were the local leaders of the church. There were about nine or
ten people at the meeting.

As the meeting started, I felt immediately as if a light of joy
went on. I was deeply moved by an opening prayer given by an old
man. I felt his sincerity and watched him and the other people in
the room during the prayer, and I observed a unique, beautiful spirit
of reverence in their faces. None of them knelt down, but it felt the
same as if they had. They looked serious but not worried, suddenly
beautiful in appearance, though with many wrinkles in their faces.

We met in the topmost level of the house. The room was clean
and neatly painted. There were only a couple of sofas and a table
with a white, beautiful cloth and a few chairs. I noticed that all the
blinds were pulled down. It was a little bit strange to me, why it
was that way in the middle of the day. Later I got an explanation. It
was a protection not to be seen by neighbors and other people from
the street. I didn't know anybody in the room except for the
Vojkůvka family. I knew little about this church, but I felt so happy
among all of these people. This is the place to be, because here I
don't have to feel ashamed while speaking about the positive things
of life. These people wouldn't laugh at the good thoughts and feelings I would share, but would take them seriously and sincerely, I
thought. I had seen this attitude of peacefulness and goodness
rarely, and only with an individual, but it was very new to me to

see it in this whole group of people who abounded with sincerity and integrity in a way I had not seen so far.

I was amazed at how much these people knew about the gospel. It felt so different from all the experiences I had in the Protestant church I remembered from my childhood. Here, a teacher started a lesson, and in a few minutes there was a great discussion. I couldn't believe how all of those faces became perfectly focused, happy, shining, optimistic—even with senses of humor. This kind of gospel is very much down to earth, I thought. I love it. It is connected to real life. Their God isn't far away for them; he is their friend with whom they converse and cooperate.

Before going back to my dormitory, I was introduced to Brother Jaromír Holcman, who would soon start to teach me the six baptismal lessons.

7

THE WATERS OF BAPTISM

I went to my first baptism lesson and was nervous. I didn't know exactly what to expect. I thought that I might be questioned on Bible history or on Jesus' life, but nothing like this happened. My first meeting with Brother Holcman took place in the middle of the week at his house. I met his wife and children, and then we started our first discussion. (I later learned that Brother Holcman's lessons were the Church's older missionary discussions from the years before the Communist takeover.) To my surprise it was really not a lesson but a discussion. Brother Holcman opened our meeting with a word of a prayer, in which he prayed for me and asked that my heart might be opened. I was touched by his words; in my entire life, I had never heard anyone pray specifically for me.

The various questions he asked me during our first discussion weren't at all easy for me to answer. I entered into a religious world of words and terms with which I wasn't familiar. These words sounded strange, uncomfortable, and foreign to me. I felt as if I were sitting in someone else's seat and not mine. While listening I realized that I had stepped into a completely different culture, language, and spiritual environment. I experienced something like a spiritual culture shock. It was exciting to hear about the plan of our

Heavenly Father, but it sounded like a fairy tale to me. I have a long way to go, I thought.

In my heart I began to deeply consider Heavenly Father as a being. It seemed impossible that I could be created in his image. I couldn't believe that he could actually be a person with a similar body to that which we humans have. His body, I learned, is perfected. But what did that mean? It sounded too simple amid this difficult universe. How was he created as a person? Does even Heavenly Father have a father? Could anything even remotely like this be possible? How will I find out?

All these questions were wrestling in my mind by the end of the first discussion, but I didn't say anything to Brother Holcman. I wasn't being hypocritical; I just needed to think things through. My mind was in a certain sense inclined to be contrary, but somehow I felt strongly inside of my heart that I was learning the truth. I had never felt that way before. It was hard to admit this, but I found it hard to learn the truth and to place it in balance between my mind and heart. In fact, I seemed to have begun a personal war between my mind and my heart. My mind was telling me, Forget about this! It's just another form of human demagoguery, with people lying to themselves in order to feel happy. But my heart was desirous to know more.

I knew I could win over my mind only when it would be able to accept peace with my heart. I felt basically positive and happy after taking a couple of the discussions, but my inner life was going through a huge transformation. Sometimes I was aware of it, other times not. I experienced some fear and wondered, What am I going to do with my life after baptism? I will be even more divided from my schoolmates than I am already. I won't have any friends. What am I going to do with my education, which is essentially opposed to what I am learning now about the gospel. Is it going to be a secret for the rest of my life? Could I be arrested for the religious beliefs I might accept? I probably could. All this and more was running through my mind almost every day.

I started to attend the Sunday meetings regularly. There would be a blessing of the sacrament, one speaker, and then Sunday school. I didn't know anything about the other Church organizations such as Priesthood, Relief Society, Young Single Adults, Primary, etc. At our meetings we didn't have an organ playing the hymns and a whole chapel singing, didn't see fathers blessing their newborn babies, didn't hear a teenager's testimony. We didn't have homemaking meetings or receive visits from visiting teachers or home teachers. The Church in my country was happy to manage a sacrament meeting every other Sunday without being noticed by the police. The more I learned about the Church, and especially about the members' lives, the more I was amazed by their endurance, faithfulness, and ability to survive daily doses of the Communists' message and still be faithful members of the Church. I heard directly from most of them, and they told me of their and their families' being constantly questioned and persecuted. I understood that many of the members had to leave the country for this reason. Many of those who stayed behind had only pictures of their sons and daughters who now lived outside of Czechoslovakia. These pictures were their entire treasures, their life and hope. Those photos were often the only connection they had with their families. Sitting among these old members felt like sitting under a beautiful tree, surrounded by long branches which gave you peace from the sharp world around you. Their deep roots, as symbols of their incredible faithfulness, were able to survive all the storms of their lives, including the Second World War and then the Communist takeover of their country and property. However, they didn't complain too much. Communist oppression was a fact of their lives that had left certain marks but didn't change their faith a bit. Sometimes it seemed their lives were stopped in the middle, and they were left only with their faith to work through to the end of their lives.

Somehow they learned to be happy in their limited circumstances, even though they were constantly watched by the many hunting dogs of Communism. They learned how to wait decades to enter the archives in their own country to find their ancestors, and they eagerly read twenty- or thirty-year-old volumes of the Church magazines, and they were as grateful for one translated sentence from a Church source as others would be for a whole book. They rejoiced in any news, cards, and letters from Salt Lake City, any written contact with other members of the Church living in freedom. These shards of the Lord's light that came to their houses as a miracle would be cherished and would produce great joy for weeks, even months and years.

I couldn't understand this very well because I didn't have the full experience they had, but what I knew was that I was learning the gospel from real heroes.

While being prepared for baptism, I learned so much from each discussion and each Sunday meeting! Every new idea of the restored gospel seemed like the discovery of a new universe, of a new light and a way of life. The doctrines that other Church members learn step by step while growing up in the Church, and therefore while there is natural time to absorb them, I was digesting within a much shorter period of time. It wasn't easy to make such a change. I had to wrestle with all the different half-true life facts which had been presented to me while I was growing up with Communism and without the gospel. Although I had never connected myself with Communist doctrines, I realized that they somehow had become a part of my environmental thinking and attitudes over the years as I had been required to listen to Communist teachings every day at school from the first grade on. They affected my way of thinking because I had breathed them in like an invisible stench in the air. They led me only to gaining a critical, cynical outlook and to a poor black-and-white way of seeing and thinking about the world. It was painful to discover this fact through my daily growth in the gospel. Nevertheless, it gave me strength to try harder to become more humble and submissive and to accept the new truth I was learning.

My life felt suddenly so rich and full on account of the new gospel ideas. That does not mean that I didn't have millions of questions and at least some doubts. I did, but I was eager to resolve them by studying the scriptures, asking questions, attending the Sunday meetings regularly, and learning how to pray.

Step by step I moved forward in my comprehension. Each discussion was a new series of heavy study material. I had one discussion every three or four weeks with Brother Holcman, and I still felt there wasn't enough time in between for me to thoroughly study or to accept and assimilate all the new gospel language and doctrines. I felt both overwhelmed and happy all at once.

A difficult point in the discussions was Joseph Smith's first vision. It was something that I had never heard before in my life. I couldn't quite absorb God's extraordinary appearance to Joseph Smith with my almost nonreligious background and with my school-gained attitude that all knowledge can be obtained only through logic and thinking. I devoted many prayers to finding a comforting and agreeable understanding of his vision. Nothing happened for weeks and months. In the beginning I thought, Well, if he could have a vision like this, why couldn't I? But it didn't work this way. I struggled. I knew that without having a testimony concerning Joseph Smith's first vision and his role as a servant of God, I couldn't be baptized. I didn't want to proceed without this essential part of a testimony. I read Joseph Smith's account of the First Vision over and over again, but I didn't feel the change of attitude I was seeking. I did believe it could have happened, but I couldn't comprehend the greatness and simplicity of this marvelous vision. It just didn't work with my mind. I wished I could know a little bit more about Joseph Smith's personality and his life, but there was no literature available to me. In the Communist encyclopedia I read

that he was a madman who was mentally ill and suffered halluci-
nations. Well, that didn't sound too encouraging, but actually, I
came to a good conclusion about that "information." I told myself,
That's great! If the Communists say something like that, they must
be afraid of something very important about the man. This
approach usually worked with any kind of searching I did in the
encyclopedia; if there were too many negative points from the
Communist point of view, there had to be something really good
and important to look for. It was like a hidden sign to me.

One day while I was reading 3 Nephi, chapter 11, which
describes the appearance of Jesus Christ in America after his resurrection, I was deeply touched and felt the Spirit. Suddenly I came
to a new and very important understanding: If I could feel such a
strong and beautiful spirit from the Book of Mormon, which was
translated by Joseph Smith, why should I question his vision? He
certainly must be a man chosen by God to be able to translate such
powerful scriptures. I knew the scriptural accounts were true, and if
they were true, Joseph Smith had to be a true prophet of God.

While I was pondering these ideas, I felt that all the reason for
my troubles with accepting Joseph Smith was that I wanted to
understand his mission from only one side—only to reach an intellectual acceptance of his mission—but I wasn't actually looking for
the real reason why he was called by God and was chosen to
restore the gospel. I felt embarrassed when I realized this about
myself. Although I did know a little about him at that point, it came
to my understanding that Joseph's heart must have been incredibly
humble, sincere, and searching for the truth in a way I had not
experienced. I realized that his humble way of searching for the
truth in the middle of all the religious confusion in which he lived
had to become also my way of trying to find out about the truth for
myself.

I knelt on my knees and felt how arrogant, foolish, and childish
I had been in my approach. To come to this personal confession

opened a door for me to learn about Joseph Smith in a completely
new way. I read his vision again. This time it felt different—as if I
were reading it for the first time, and with a pure motivation—to
find out the truth. Not only did I read his words but this time I was
able to absorb Joseph's spirit of sincerity and truthfulness as he
described his experiences. My mind was clear and unclouded by
doubts, and now, with its new openness, my heart was able to res-
onate with the purity of his testimony. I knew that this man was
telling the truth and that his testimony was real—an important part
of the foundation of the restored gospel on the earth. I received this
knowledge with an assurance of my whole soul, with a complete
unity of mind and heart. I discovered a new way of pondering,
thinking, and searching for answers to my questions. I felt different because suddenly I realized that there was a completely opposite thinking process needed in order to obtain answers to my
questions. It was a much more complete and deeper way of thinking than just using my brain alone. I knew that this way of searching was connected to the sincerity and purity of my heart. The more
I realized this truth, the more I desired to be baptized and cleansed
from my sins.

I was so happy after receiving the answer about Joseph Smith's
vision. A very important key to my baptism was now in my pos-
session, and I knew from that time on what it felt like to have and
to bear a testimony. Whenever I had heard some member of the
Church bear his or her testimony before I had obtained my own,
the word *testimony* sounded so strange—almost like part of a court-
room drama. Why do people have to testify about the truth of the
Church? I asked myself, not able to understand and appreciate it.
However, after I received my own understanding of the reality of
the First Vision and the truthfulness of the restored gospel, I recognized the necessity of this act of faith. The spirit of truth so strongly
resonated in my heart that sharing my own experience of obtaining
a testimony and identifying myself with any new knowledge about

the restored gospel was now vital and essential to my life—like my own breath. The strong manifestation of the Spirit that accompanies newly obtained truth always awakens my heart, brain, and my whole spiritual being. To decide not to share it feels like wasting the most precious part of myself. Every newly expressed part of my personal testimony became a milestone of my eternal progress.

The last discussion in preparation for my baptism was held in the middle of January, and I learned from Brother Holcman that because the Church didn't have a baptismal font in Brno, I would need to wait for half a year to be baptized. The nearest baptismal season would be the next summer. It wasn't a disappointment to me. On the contrary, I felt that I would have more time to prepare myself for this most important step in my life.

I was rereading the Book of Mormon, and I loved the experience of reading it a second time. These wonderful scriptures became a path to my repentance and change of my heart. At that time I was living at a student dormitory, so I was careful to read the Book of Mormon only when my roommates were away. I didn't feel comfortable reading the book in any other public place; it would be too dangerous if someone found out that I owned the book. My university studies would no doubt end at that moment. But although I knew I had to keep my reading a secret, I was also aware that I had found a very precious thing in my life.

I didn't tell anyone about my new discovery. I didn't even tell my parents about attending the church meetings on Sundays. At the time, I felt that they lived in a different world than the one I was discovering in Brno. I didn't think it was possible to explain to them what I was preparing for. I felt they would think I was crazy and they would worry for my safety and my university studies.

Further, I knew I would have to prepare them before sharing my new belief with them. They would have to see through my actions, school grades, and behavior that I was becoming a different and better person. Words alone wouldn't convince them. Only my acts could testify for me. Moreover, I realized that there were not any members of the Church in my hometown and that I would be the very first Latter-day Saint there.

At that time my parents had not attended any church for years and generally weren't interested in religion. They were very good, hardworking, and humble people, but the harshness of Communism painted its own design in their lives, as in everyone else's in my country. Because they had learned through years of Communist government how to manage their lives within all the limits they faced every day, they were generally happy. However, they didn't show much excitement for the future. I knew they loved their children and saw in them their only future hope. I was the only one from my family who had applied for the university, and I knew that they had high hopes for me.

"You have been a pioneer since you were a child," my mom always used to say to me. When I started to study at the university she would add, "Oli, we can give you a lot, but I know that we have our limits. But our limits cannot become yours. Don't forget that. You are a new line in our family."

She would occasionally take my hands in hers and would tell me with tears in her eyes, "Sometimes I wonder what good we have done that we deserve such a good daughter as you!" These words always made me really uncomfortable, and I didn't understand them. But when I found the Church and understood a little bit more about the purpose of my life, I was deeply moved by this mother's testimony, and wondered how it was possible that I was blessed with such great parents who were yet so humble—who even looked up to their daughter, although I wasn't a perfect kid. I felt that my parents trusted me completely, and I trusted them in the same way. I knew that when I got baptized I would do anything to make it possible for my parents to learn about the restored gospel. They deserved so much in return for the goodness of their hearts. I just wondered how they, at that time in their early sixties, would respond to this news of my following a new religion.

July 11, 1982, arrived, and the day of my baptism was now a reality. I fasted the whole day. A small meeting was held before the baptism on Saturday evening. Only Brother Holcman, his wife, and both the younger and the older Brother Vojkůvka were present at the baptismal meeting held at the Holcmans' house.

I arrived early that day at Brother Holcman's house. I had waited so long for this day, I was excited and felt really ready for this step. It was wonderful to feel joy and happiness with this small congregation. I felt how much they loved me and respected my decision to be baptized. We had this meeting late in the evening, and at about ten o'clock at night we went by car to a reservoir near the city of Brno.

As soon as we arrived at the place, we had a short prayer in the car. Now I learned firsthand of the real circumspection of these Czech Latter-day Saint brethren. First, the younger Brother Vojkůvka went to check the situation at the spot where I would be baptized. He came back within ten minutes or so and told us that there were a few fishermen there, but we would probably be all right. I took my bag with the baptismal clothes, and Brother Holcman's wife came along to help me, although she wasn't a member of the Church and had never seen a baptism before. We came to the place the brethren had picked, made a circle, and held hands while one of the brothers offered a prayer. We couldn't see each other because of the darkness of the night, and we whispered even the prayer.

The other brethren were about to go to check the water's edge when we suddenly heard men's voices. There was silence among us, since we didn't know who those men were. Were they policemen or tourists or just someone coming to have fun? Younger Brother Vojkůvka instructed us to walk together but not as a group, always just two or three together. I was in suspense as we waited for him to walk near the men and learn why they were there. Finally he came back and told us that the men were fishermen checking for a good spot for fishing. The men, talking loudly to each other, sat at the water's edge for ten minutes, twenty minutes. None of us knew what their plan would be.

"The water's edge is pretty steep at most places here. This is the only place we know of that has a gradual and safe descent into the water," Brother Vojkůvka said almost to himself.

We waited and waited. I leaned my head against the trunk of a tree and felt hopeless. Maybe I am not prepared enough, or my testimony isn't strong enough, or I haven't fully repented, I thought. I could still hear the fishermen's voices. I was about to kneel down in prayer when Brother Holcman came to me, took me by the arms, and walked me toward the other members of our small baptismal group.

"I think we need to pray again to make it possible for Olga to be baptized today," he said. He asked us to kneel down and hold hands, and he offered a prayer. I couldn't see the tears in his eyes, but I could feel his voice whispering the prayer in the most humble way I have ever witnessed. "Please, Heavenly Father, make it possible for Olga to be baptized today, if it is thy will," he asked.

After the prayer we held hands and could still hear the fishermen's voices, but within a minute or so, they suddenly stood up and left. It was a miracle for me. The water was quiet and peaceful at that moment.

Brother Holcman, who would baptize me that night, entered the water first, and then he walked back toward the water's edge where I was waiting and took my right hand, walking with me as we went deeper into the water. I felt at that very moment that everything was changed in my life. I strongly felt the power of the priesthood for the first time in my life—it felt like a safeness and an unshakable authority to act in the name of God. Brother Holcman offered the baptismal prayer, and when I heard my name I felt in

my whole body and spirit that I had ended one lengthy chapter of
my life. While walking back out of the water, I felt a complete joy
in every pore of my being. I knew that this baptism was recorded in
heaven. It was a real act, not only a ceremony to enjoy and to see.

That evening, on the way back in Brother Holcman's car, I
heard for the first time in my life the music of the Mormon
Tabernacle Choir. I felt exactly as if I were listening to angels in
heaven. I was thrilled when Brother Holcman told me that this
choir consisted of hundreds of members of the Church. It was
impossible to feel alone among so many members and their beautiful voices, even though the music was only on a tape. Their
voices, filled with the Spirit of God, penetrated my heart in the
middle of the night, and I pondered what their lives must be like in
the heart of the Church in beautiful Salt Lake City, blessed with a
living prophet, apostles, and a free country.

I was confirmed that same night. I had never seen before the
laying on of hands. As soon as the brethren laid their hands upon
my head and pronounced me a member of The Church of Jesus
Christ of Latter-day Saints, I knew that the old spirit of loneliness
and confusion was gone, and I felt fully accepted by God into his
kingdom as one of his daughters. Receiving the Holy Ghost
brought me a most beautiful assurance that I didn't have to be lost
in the confused world. The companionship of the Holy Ghost felt
like the sweet embrace of a best friend. My whole body felt completely cleansed and renewed to a life of happiness and joy. Above
all, I was awakened in my spirit, and I felt on my baptismal day as
if I had renewed a lost connection to the eternal part of my being.

The most amazing thing to me was when I heard in the prayer
of confirmation that I would be able to bring multitudes into the
Church. I thought about this all the time from that day on. This sentence particularly became my personal Liahona for my direction
and activity in the Church for the coming years while living in
Czechoslovakia.

CHAPTER

8

UNDERGROUND
MISSIONARY WORK

One of my strongest desires right after my baptism was to share my happiness and joy with others. Although I was a new member and the only young person in the small Brno branch, I could already see more clearly than ever before what my family, closest friends, and the whole country had been suffering from: an insufficiency of love, sense of purpose, and inner peace. It was clear to me that others, too, needed the light of the gospel in their lives. However, I couldn't simply go up to my friends and family and start talking about the gospel. My family would worry about me, and my friends would think I was insane.

The Church of Jesus Christ of Latter-day Saints was not recognized by the Communist government, and Czech people knew nothing about Mormons. If I talked to people about the restored gospel directly, they wouldn't understand what I was talking about because they didn't even know anything about the teachings of any of the already-existing churches in the country. However, the more I realized this truth around me, the more I dreamed, prayed, and thought about the best, safest, and most effective way to share the restored truth with my fellowmen in Communist Czechoslovakia. The scripture "With God all things are possible" (Matthew 19:26) took on special meaning for me. There has to be a way to do missionary work, I thought.

As I sat in Sunday meetings with our congregation of a handful of Czech Saints in the city of Brno each week, I felt as if we were one family, and there was a beautiful spirit. Yet my heart was also sad as I wondered, How can I be fully happy if I cannot share this with others? This was a constant question in my mind. It was like rejoicing with a wonderful but closed society of great people who had earned treasures of knowledge, truth, and happiness but could not let any of this beauty past their door to the tough Communist world waiting just outside.

Because of their association with the Church before the Communist takeover, all these beautiful members were known as Mormons by the government and therefore were constantly watched and regularly questioned by the secret police. The Church was not recognized by the Communist government at that time, and therefore any public activity, not to mention missionary work, would mean more danger to the members' lives and families. They had to be unbelievably careful to meet only on Sundays, and even then, our Sunday meetings were held in secret so as not to alarm the secret police. Many of the members couldn't even come every Sunday because they would be followed by someone on the street on their way to the meeting.

The only other outside contact our small congregation had was with the Saints who lived in Prague, and this was usually only once or twice a year. Brother Jiří Šnederfler, who presided over the group of Prague Saints and the entire Czech Church, would occasionally come to visit us in Brno, but except for him we were very much alone.

To my knowledge, I was the only young, new member in the Brno area. Up to that point, the secret police knew nothing about my religious affiliation. That was my great advantage. It gave me a freedom of activity and movement not possible for the older brothers and sisters in the branch, some of whom had been Church members for the entire forty years of the Church's existence in Czechoslovakia and all of whom were constantly watched and persecuted.

I talked with Brother Otakar Vojkůvka about my desire to share the gospel. He knew that missionary work was always on the top of my discussion agenda after I got baptized. I wanted to know if he could see any way that we could unofficially make some efforts to spread the gospel or to at least prepare people for the gospel in Czechoslovakia, even within our tight and limited restraints.

"One possibility has occurred to me, Olga. You could become a yoga teacher and help spread the gospel by first preparing learners with some physical discipline through yoga principles, coupled with mental preparation through carefully introducing them to some gospel truths," he responded.

Although it sounded very strange at first, I quickly realized that his idea made sense. That was, after all, exactly the way I had first come into contact with Brother Vojkůvka and later the Czech Saints.

"I cannot start speaking about the Church directly, but I can influence others to do at least some good for themselves and their families," I agreed.

"Olga, people are and always will be concerned about their health. That's why yoga would be a useful approach to start with. Later on you can add more," he continued.

I applied for yoga teacher training the very next day. Although yoga was also watched by the Communists because of its origins in the Hindu religion, officials did not object to people's practicing a part of the yoga system called hatha yoga, which focuses only on the physical benefits of doing yoga postures.

As soon as I completed my yoga teacher training I approached a sports club in my hometown. They hadn't had any yoga programs there before. They didn't even know what I was talking about in the beginning. I wasn't successful when I returned the next week with the hope of negotiating a contract for teaching.

"We don't have any room available for yoga—try next year," was the short answer from the head of the sports club. On my way out I was asked to fill out some papers for "possible future yoga teaching." While I was doing so, I was interrupted by one of the secretaries who was working in the office.

"Oh, I have a terrible headache," she said.

"When did it start?" I asked.

"Early this morning," she answered.

"It looks like you have a lot of paper work to do," I said while looking at a couple of big piles sitting on her desk.

"Oh, yes, and it's due today. I've already taken four aspirin and they haven't helped me," she continued.

"Well, I know a few exercises that might help your headache," I said, surprising myself a little bit.

"What's that?" she asked, not knowing that I was applying to teach yoga at the club.

"I can show you. Can I open the window and can you find a comfortable chair to sit on?" I said, hatching a plan on the fly. There was terrible smoke from cigarettes—a common European bad habit. I showed her a few exercises. She repeated them after me. A few secretaries passed through the office, looked at us with confused faces, and left the office.

"How are you feeling?" I asked the secretary after ten minutes of working with her.

"I feel much better. I still have a headache but it is much milder than a few minutes ago," she answered. I continued and explained to her what would be good to do when the pain came again.

"Oh, it feels so good. I am feeling that my headache is really going away. Where did you learn this?" the secretary asked me. I told her about yoga. To my surprise, she called the other secretaries into her office, and I held something like my very first yoga miniconference. I explained briefly what yoga was about, showed them a few exercises, and asked them to follow me. Not all of them did, but afterwards I could see that they were really excited about the whole idea.

"This is great! We should have something like this here. Everybody would feel much better," they said. I explained to them that that was actually the reason I had come to the club, but because of lack of rooms I had been delayed until next year. The secretaries said they were certain they could help me find a place to hold the classes, and they asked me to bring my written yoga schedule, an outline of all the lessons, and a description of the course, and they would help me.

In a few weeks I gave my first public yoga lecture at the local gymnasium. The sports club even made flyers for me, and I was thrilled at the power of a few capable and enthusiastic secretaries. About fifty people attended this lecture, and I got permission a week later to open yoga classes in Uherské Hradiště, my home-town. It came in handy that the head of the sports club learned I was studying physical education at the university. However, he still saw fit to send a few secret police to my classes to check me out. I found out very easily who they were. They smelled of cigarettes and were too lazy to perform any exercises. This would be an obvi-ous sign to me from the beginning to help me distinguish them from others, who were eager and happy to learn about yoga.

First, I opened a two-month yoga course just to see the reac-tion in my hometown. I was amazed to see that each lesson was attended by more and more new students. The word spread quickly, and I had to offer a second yoga course a couple of months later, to my great surprise! Each class began with about forty partici-pants.

"Can I still enroll in your class? Isn't it too late?" I would hear after I had already taught a month of a new course. I would smile and reply, "It's never too late!" The gym was pretty much full, within a month of a new session, with yoga students as far as the eye could see.

People from all different age groups participated in the classes: teenagers, university students, working people, and many of retirement age. I had never had the chance to work with such an age variety before. In the beginning I thought that it might create some problems, but the opposite was true. Everybody did exercises on his or her own level. I was trying to teach them not to compare themselves to others, which is the first yoga principle. They liked that a lot, as it was unique for them to hear that they didn't have to follow some mob ideal but instead meet the needs of their own body and mind. For many people that principle was like a new discovery or even a revelation. They realized that their own bodies and minds were able to teach them more about themselves. After exercises people would stay seated on their blankets. I would ask them to come closer and create a small circle where I would present a small lecture. They weren't comfortable sitting next to each other and often I had to invite them again to come closer. They weren't used to gathering except for boring Communist party meetings, and I could see their disbelief, doubt, and fear in the beginning. But after a few lessons they would sit together without any problem and would even respond to a few of my questions.

I planned every single activity for a purpose. First, I knew that they had to feel comfortable with me and with each other in the class. Second, I wanted to ease any fear they might possibly have of each other in order to let them feel free to share some of their ideas regarding the class. Also, I thought that it was important that they come to the class not only as individuals but as part of a larger whole.

I had to be careful not to talk about any subject that could raise some doubts about continuing with the classes. It was impossible to mention publicly the Bible, Jesus, or the name of God. It would indeed mean the end of my efforts. I just talked about physical and mental health. I could see how hungry people were just to listen to positive ideas. My traditional yoga lesson would consist of sixty minutes of exercises, ending with ten minutes of relaxation, and then I would give the small lecture afterwards for about a half hour. Some people left the class right after the hatha yoga session, but the majority stayed for the lecture as well. I realized that there were even some people who came only to listen to the lecture but didn't participate in hatha yoga. That was a good sign to me that I was on the right track to being able to provide something meaningful. By the end of the first year I had two full yoga groups and was teaching about one hundred people total. The third year my classes met in two large gyms instead of the small one I had been using. That was a great sign.

Even the sports club benefitted directly from the yoga classes, because each yoga student automatically became a member of the sports club. In the following years, yoga students increased the membership of the small club enormously, and I was suddenly treated with great respect by the sports boss and even was given a sports teacher's award after five years of teaching yoga. As I accepted the award, I smiled broadly as I thought, If only you knew!

Fridays, my yoga class days, became my busiest days of the week. I would finish my school classes in Brno in the morning and then take the next bus to go home and teach yoga in Uherské Hradiště. I didn't realize in the beginning that this work within the gym walls would become a firm foundation of missionary activity for more than ten years under the Communist regime and would come to involve a number of other young members who would join the Church later and become yoga teachers/missionaries like me.

I eventually learned how to approach positive and slightly spiritual topics without using religious words, while still being accepted by the listeners. I learned to support my ideas with quotes from many great Russian and other Eastern European poets and writers and even some Marxist-Leninist philosophers whose ideas I learned at the university, along with some ideas from Russian politicians and leaders. Here and there even the politicians, especially after Gorbachev came to power, would say "by accident" something meaningful which could become a good supporting idea for the more serious topics I was trying to introduce. I could see satisfaction in people's faces as I offered them something different and positive. I noticed that the secret police yoga participants always raised their eyebrows when I mentioned some Russian politician. They no doubt anticipated my saying something politically wrong, and instead they often looked shocked when I applied Gorbachev's ideas, for example, in a positive way, to life in my country. A few people understood my effort quickly and liked it because it actually felt safe: they took my commentary as a good political joke—a way of balancing the Communists' unbalanced way of thinking. I even saw some Communists come to my classes—not watching or spying on me but actually taking the classes seriously. When I talked to them after classes, I realized that even they were hungry for a different food than that offered to them at their party meetings. It made me smile. Once it even happened to me that a Communist who was taking one of my yoga sessions came to me and asked me if I wouldn't mind giving a lesson at the party meeting. I thought he was joking, but when he pulled out the schedule of upcoming party meetings, I knew he was serious. I mentioned that he had been attending my class for three years and asked him why he himself wouldn't present the lesson.

"Nobody would believe a word of it from me," he said.

"Why do you think that they would have reason to believe me?" I asked him.

"Well, they wouldn't believe you either, but I thought it might be a good idea to bring them at least some meaningful subject matter!"

I politely declined his offer and apologized. I wasn't sure then, and still don't know today, whether it was some kind of provocation on his part or a naive but sincere idea.

Soon after I started the first months of classes, people began coming to me first with health problems and later on with personal problems. I was twenty years old and was surprised at how much these adults and older people trusted me, a young person. Above all, it gave me a unique opportunity to work with people on an individual level, naturally creating a good chance to be a little bit more specific in my discussions, though I still had to be careful with my suggestions.

The next teaching year I assumed that the classes would go more or less as in the first year. To my surprise, about two hundred people signed up for the class, and I found myself teaching four yoga classes. Seeing a need for other yoga teachers in future years, I asked a few young students who attended yoga classes regularly if they would be interested in becoming yoga teachers in the future. They were very excited about the idea. I introduced them to Brother Vojkůvka to make sure they would get the right idea about yoga teaching. I hoped they would feel the Spirit, seek the truth, and become members of the Church as I had done. Indeed, two young brothers, Petr and Marek Kasan, became yoga teachers and joined the Church a few months after they began teaching. Others followed them. I was still the only person giving lectures after yoga sessions; the newly baptized Church members didn't feel adequate to do so for a certain period of time.

When others told me they were afraid to speak and that giving the lectures seemed easy for me, like second nature, I told them of the example of Brother Otakar Vojkůvka, a great teacher in this instance. He was always a great speaker who didn't put anyone in the audience to sleep as he presented skills and ideas that people in my country lacked. He was familiar with a lot of good foreign literature and was a great example of basic missionary skills.

My years of teaching yoga were a wonderful time for me. I

was studying the gospel and making plans to somehow continue to do my part in helping people find truth in the unique Czech environment of atheistic thinking and Communism.

Missionary work became my main "calling," although it didn't actually exist as an official calling within the Czech Church at that time. For that matter, the Church didn't exist publicly. Doing missionary work became second nature to me because a desire to share the gospel was pumping through every fiber of my soul. Words and prayers couldn't begin to express my joy when another of my friends or yoga students was baptized into the Church. The older members were also thrilled to see new members coming into the Church. They sometimes said, perhaps not fully realizing the prophetic nature of their words, "A new era is coming in the Church in Czechoslovakia."

9

A Small Army of God

Brother Otakar Vojkůvka had a great missionary heart, and he always brought new vision to the problems of strengthening baptized members and, within our limits, sharing the gospel with others. After a few yoga students, most of them university students, were baptized, they opened yoga classes in their universities and hometowns. We would have informal planning meetings with Brother Vojkůvka almost every week on how to progress with our goals of preparing others to receive the gospel. When I mentioned the need for more opportunities to discuss with yoga students principles that would prepare them for receiving the gospel, Brother Vojkůvka knew exactly what to do: "We need summer yoga camps, and you have to organize them."

I was overwhelmed, but we sat down that evening and listed ideas for organizing it. We decided to invite to the camps people from the different yoga courses our young Church members had begun teaching all over Czechoslovakia. We knew that only those who were deeply interested in our yoga lessons would spend one week of their precious vacation at a camp like this. That gave us the hope that we would have a more narrowly focused group of people, exactly what we were looking for. We started off that first summer with five rounds of yoga camps, each of them starting on a Sunday evening and finishing the next Saturday. This schedule gave all the members of the Church the opportunity to worship the Lord on Sundays. Each camp leader would attend sacrament meeting in the morning, along with Sunday school, and would then rest in preparation for the next course.

We planned our entire yoga camp enterprise very carefully with Brother Vojkůvka. Our goal was to help prepare Czech people to accept the gospel if they had the opportunity in the future. We knew we wouldn't be able to teach the gospel directly in the camps, but we wanted to create such a program and atmosphere that the people who attended would hunger and thirst for more knowledge about the purpose of their lives. We wanted them to wonder about the spirit they would experience in these camps so they could eventually learn to experience this in the purest way possible—as Latter-day Saints.

More than ninety percent of the camp participants would be atheists. We knew this before we started. Therefore, we realized that our steps toward spiritual topics had to be careful and small, like a bird's hop. We knew that the first step would be just to teach people to learn how to feel good about themselves as human beings and to give them some sense of enthusiasm for life. Further, we knew that participants at yoga camps wouldn't be coming to hear the gospel. They wouldn't even know what the word meant, and therefore, it would be a great mistake to use the yoga idea only as bait and then start talking suddenly about the gospel. We were ethically obligated to offer them exactly what they came for—a yoga camp.

Further, any overt attempt at religious activities would mean real danger, as religion was a strictly forbidden public topic in Communist Czechoslovakia. Because we knew little about the backgrounds of those who filled out the yoga camp application, we could easily end up having to close the camp very suddenly because of a police notice from an irate camp participant. We knew these things had happened in the past with other people who had tried to secretly teach religion in the country. They were persecuted and questioned by the police without ceasing. We thought of several ways in which to introduce gospel principles to the people without using the name of the Church or even the name of God. We could not read or quote any kind of scriptures in public speeches; that was considered religious preaching and was strictly forbidden by the government. To read from the scriptures in public was to literally admit yourself to the nearest prison. The police would be at the place sooner than you could finish your talk. Therefore, if we were to talk about being kind to others, we could never once add "as Jesus always did." People who were listening carefully and knew at least a little bit about Jesus' teachings could read between our lines, but the other listeners wouldn't have any clue that we were referring to certain scriptures from the New Testament.

The yoga courses we taught during the school year served as resources for finding potential camp participants. We decided to hold the camps in the summer, when young college students could take time off to join us or work for us. Then we began looking for a place to hold the camps. After much searching, we settled on a small village named Radňovice (whose name appropriately and accidentally means Joyville), and rented a building that had a kitchen, a main dining and meeting hall, two large rooms for sleeping, and bathrooms. It had a grassy patch in front, ideal for yoga excercising, and it was surrounded by farmland and woods.

We knew that our first goal would be to open their minds, wake up and stretch them after the physical and mental lethargy of the dismal Communist lifestyle. We planned a very strict camp schedule. Nobody could smoke or drink alcohol. All of them were politely but directly asked the first day they arrived to follow the entire schedule of the day, especially the evening curfew. We felt strongly while preparing the camp program that if we established a solid foundation of decency, friendship, and order, the Spirit of God could prevail.

For this purpose it was also convenient that yoga deals with perfection of the body, stability of the mind, and clarity of the intellect. People with whom we worked generally needed their physical health improved, but also because of the Communist system their mind was filled with fear, doubts, and general unhappiness. As they listened to our yoga lectures, they realized they could find their own identity in the world and not feel like a small, unimportant clove of garlic pressed down into its own juice on a daily basis. Just to teach them how to sleep better, relax, improve memory, and concentrate better on daily tasks through physical yoga exercises was a revelation for many of them. They saw that they could be responsible for their own happiness or misery despite the state of affairs in the country in which they lived.

All these ideas were the foundation of what we began doing at our summer camps. As soon as the people arrived and were accommodated, we would give a first lecture wherein we would introduce our goals for the week. There were four points we usually talked about. First, we said that we wanted to achieve general purity and cleanness. We emphasized that we would work to develop a purity of the mind and clean ourselves from the things binding us and keeping us from feeling happiness and joy in our everyday lives. Second, we told them we would try to introduce what real personal freedom is about. Third, we would try to cultivate beauty in our activities during the week. Fourth, we would work on everyone's progress toward perfection, which we introduced as understanding the truth about life and finding out why we are here, what is the purpose of our lives, and what our future is all about.

The food was very simply planned. For the first three days of camp we would eat a cleansing wheat diet which consisted of boiled and sprouted wheat, raw fruit, steamed vegetables, and lots of water.

The simple, meatless meals had a purpose—to bring a bit of physical discipline to participants. The first days of camp were difficult: some participants were tired, others would have headaches or feel sleepy. Usually after the first two days, however, people would feel much better physically as well as emotionally. Above all, most participants, accustomed to eating pork meat and sausages almost every day, felt a sense of accomplishment after having observed such a strict diet regimen successfully. Some of them even wanted to continue the restrictive wheat diet for another day or two. During the remainder of the camp, the menu featured simple meatless foods like milk, baked potatoes, fresh bread, and vegetable soups.

Although we couldn't mention God, much less pray before meals, we held hands before each meal, gathering into a large, fifty-person circle. Either Brother Vojkůvka or one of us Latter-day Saint camp leaders would publicly express gratitude in this manner: "Dear friends, let us hold our hands, calm our minds, and close our eyes to express our gratitude for the hands which prepared this beautiful food. Let us remember our families, fellow citizens and friends, and send them an idea of peace and joy in their lives. Let us think about other people in the world who suffer hunger or unhappiness, and send them the idea of love. Let everyone on this earth be happy." Instead of saying amen, we would simply say "Dobrou chuť" (good appetite), then offer the person on our left and right a special "good appetite." The majority of people were very uncomfortable doing this in the first few days of camp, but we still offered our thanks before every meal, three times a day. Some participants tried to avoid this before-meals ceremony, but we wouldn't start until everybody was present. Interestingly, many families who participated at the camps brought this tradition home and continued to give thanks for their meals.

Camp participants helped prepare meals by cleaning or chopping fruits and vegetables, and they also helped clean the rooms, halls, and gathering places. We worked together to clean the wheat before boiling it, removing any small stones or weeds as one would do with rice, lentils, or beans. While we were gathered together sifting the wheat, we would sing Czech folk songs and read Czech fables. We did this exercise usually on the beginning day of the course, and helped us to build a good starting point among people who didn't know each other. This activity would take about three hours, but it rendered great social as well as culinary benefits. Singing was always a main part of our camp program. For Czech people, singing comes as naturally as a baby's first breath. If there was a cold feeling at the beginning of the camp among the people, we would always start singing. Within a few minutes of absorbing a few Bohemian, Moravian, and Slovak folk songs, the group would radiate with a warm spirit of friendship and joy.

There were three one-and-a-half-hour hatha yoga exercise sessions daily. The first started at six o'clock in the morning, in the open air, so that we could welcome the sunrise.

After the morning yoga class and a healthy breakfast, we would have a lecture from nine to eleven o'clock. The mornings were usually devoted to various health topics. We talked about managing stress, getting rid of headaches, prevention measures that help avoid various illnesses, and also other topics more generally related to the human body: laziness, too much or too little sleep, healthy diet habits, self-discipline, etc. After the lesson was the second hour and a half of hatha yoga practice, and then the morning schedule ended with a light lunch. After lunch the participants would have about three hours for their own personal needs and enjoyment.

We gathered again as a group at three in the afternoon and continued with a lesson focused more on human relationships: how to create a better family atmosphere at home; how to deal with arguing, jealousy, anger, excessive caution in life, sadness, selfishness; how to teach children good moral principles; and even how to find a good life partner for marriage. Although these topics might sound normal, even slightly sleep-inducing, to an American, the reality in Czechoslovakia was very different. People knew nothing or very little about these areas of life. The Communists did not offer any meaningful books on topics like these. They allowed the public only a paltry number of books focused on human relationships, and the books were so plain and useless that no one would waste their time reading them. There was always so much Communist propaganda inside these books that I would turn from my reading in disgust and want to throw the book into the nearest garbage can. In contrast, people listened attentively to our camp lessons, taking as many notes as their hands could write, even taping lectures for their own future listening. Brother Vojkůvka was the source of all these topics; his admirable home library was a treasure trove of literature from all over the world. If I was interested in any topic, any one at all, I could always find books in his library to get me started.

The afternoon lesson was followed by another hour of practicing yoga, then dinner and a brief rest. Around seven o'clock in the evening we would take our blankets and go to watch the sunset, gathering together in a meeting very similar to a church fireside. Surrounded by the beauties of nature, we shared some ideas which we had carefully developed beforehand and which we called the "Seven Spiritual Vitamins." Each evening we introduced one of them.

This gathering, which we called *satsang,* was the most important part of the whole day from a missionary point of view, as it was often the only place where we could enter carefully into a gospel topic. Why was this possible? Because we spoke at these meetings about things that really mattered in life. We started the meeting with a song, which we considered our camp anthem, a song well known throughout the world: "We Shall Overcome."

We continued the meeting with a discussion of one of the "seven spiritual vitamins," as we called them: "admiration for good things in life," "self-respect," "interest in living," "finding joy in living," "expressing gratitude," "loving others," and "enthusiasm— finding the burning within." Evenings always represented a spiritual highlight of the day for everyone, but especially the members of the Church, because we focused the speeches on Jesus' teachings. Although we couldn't mention his name directly, we presented short quotes from the scriptures without identifying the source.

Everybody got a paper bag at the end of the first day, which would serve as a personal mailbox for the week. People were asked to list briefly the things they would like to achieve personally during the week. The bags hung on a wall of the main hall where we usually gathered for lectures, so that everyone could drop a note to someone during the day. We asked them to focus on the spiritual vitamin in such a way as to be able to express it to at least five people during the following day, either by spoken or written means. Our goal was to generate actions of service among the people, to develop a more cooperating and sharing spirit. The first days were always a hard start for everyone, and during those days the Church members/camp leaders wrote most of the notes. However, within a couple days people would start writing to each other. As a result, many great relationships were established and people started to be more open with each other.

It usually always took about three days before people would actually speak to each other in group meetings. In the beginning of the camp they would sit on their chairs without saying a word to the person sitting next to them. It was hard to figure out how they felt. We knew that each camp activity, from holding hands before every meal or to listening to lectures about human relations, was new to them. Later on, most of them confessed that they thought in the beginning that we were playing some tricks on them. People couldn't believe that there could possibly be a way to try to be happy in reality. However, when they saw our efforts as organizers of the camp and when they could actually relate to the things spoken by the first few brave souls who shared their feelings, the rest of the group would slowly come to the understanding that at this camp it was possible to be happy in a very practical sense.

Brother Vojkůvka always challenged each yoga camp participant to understand that the week they were going to spend there would be the happiest week in their lives thus far. People didn't laugh at his statement, but their faces testified of their general disbelief. It seemed they sometimes joined in the camp activities with an ironic, scornful, and sour attitude. However, as the week continued, we tried to help them see that happiness isn't something that comes from the outside world but rather from our hearts. Some people thought we were just nuts when we continued to be cheerful whether or not the weather was good, whether or not the local police came, as they occasionally did, to check us out and threaten to close our camp for some reason they would make up, hoping to get rid of us. To participants' surprise, however, we didn't alter our cheerful attitude even when things got really bad.

One challenge we faced frequently was the camp participants' questions about our bad government and about Communism in general. "Why should I be happy when the environment is so bad!" they would ask. "I cannot travel abroad or buy what I need, newspapers lie to me every day, and people who are irresponsible lead my city," others commented. These questions and comments came up naturally because our camp philosophy was based on a positive way of thinking and living. The government brought just the opposite outlook to their lives. Therefore, people saw our ideas as fairy tales, too positive and cheerful in comparison to the life they experienced. Yes, we as members of the Church felt the same questions in our hearts as these people. Brother Vojkůvka would usually answer those critical questions in a very smooth manner: "Change first yourself and then help your family, and thus you will bring more harmony and love into your own family. The biggest mistake of all of us is that we think we can change something outside in the world without changing ourselves first."

"How can my life or my family's life cause a big difference in my country?" they would ask.

"You would be surprised what a good family can achieve as a whole," he would simply say. He usually recited an old proverb at the end of such an exchange: "Plant an idea and you will harvest an action. Plant an action and you will harvest your character. Plant your character and you will harvest your whole destiny."

Of course, some people weren't satisfied with his answer and wanted to hear that the government was bad and had to change first. But we knew our limits. It was true that we had to bite our lips in situations like this, but we knew it was necessary for each of us to remain faithful to the twelfth article of faith by being subject to our government leaders and by "obeying, honoring, and sustaining the law." Many times we closed a difficult discussion with the words, "We aren't here to discuss these political things, but rather to improve our own lives by focusing on what we can change within ourselves. We believe that only the change which comes through transformation of an individual's heart can provide true happiness in our families and in the future of our nation and society." People usually didn't say much to that, but we knew that even this simple idea could bring a lot of them to a new viewpoint and a more uplifting attitude in contrast to their usual hopelessness about life in Czechoslovakia.

We faced a different kind of challenge when, after a few days of a camp session, some people would start speaking either to a fellow camper or to the whole group about their lives—personal things, family or work problems—and would want some advice to resolve them. Some participants discussed bad relationships they were experiencing, and others talked about public figures who were exercising their power unjustly, especially the Communists in leadership positions. We as camp organizers were not equipped to deal with these concerns. We had no training in the field of psychology, and we did not run the camp with the idea of our acting as personal counselors. But we felt an obligation to help people meet their individual challenges by teaching them the life principles we had learned through studying the gospel. In the first years of camps, it was usually only Brother Vojkůvka who would counsel them, but eventually people began turning even to us younger Church members for help.

That was a great life school for me—to learn to listen to people without any prejudice and to try to honestly give them some worthwhile ideas for problem solving. It seemed strange to me that someone thirty or forty years older than I would ask me, "Olga, would you help me to resolve a problem with my disobedient son?" or "Would you know how to teach my husband not to go to the pub every day?" or "Would you help me to stop smoking?" I was startled by the sincerity of these people and couldn't quite understand why they came to ask me, just a university student with much smaller life experience than they had. "Whatever you say to me will mean a great deal for my life," some said. I was amazed to hear such statements, and during the time I spent with people at camp, I prayed constantly that I might have the Spirit's guidance in those situations. I discovered that a great part of my ability to help others was in my constant spirit of repentance. Each day I knelt down and prayed to Heavenly Father to forgive me of all my imperfections and mistakes I might have made. When I did this faithfully, I would always feel the strong spirit of the Holy Ghost, and helping someone by accepting the guidance of the Spirit was much easier than doing it on my own with my limited personal level of knowledge. It was a beautiful feeling to be an instrument in the hand of the Lord, and later on I realized that it was one of the greatest gifts that Heavenly Father gave me while doing missionary work.

Usually, I stayed in touch with camp participants during the year by correspondence. That would give me some time to develop a good relationship with them and share more ideas about the gospel at next summer's camps. After a few years of putting on the camps, my mailbox was constantly jammed with letters, and yet I could only answer about twenty letters per week. Saturdays became my writing days.

Among the people in the camp there would be here and there Communist party members. These were usually the ones who had entered the party because of some kind of necessity—to help their children to get into school, to overcome a "bad" capitalist family background, or because they had joined the Communist party years ago, excited about the party's promises, and then could never annul their membership. They weren't what we in Czechoslovakia called "convinced Communists."

It was interesting to see how these people revealed themselves at the camp. They would usually come up to us alone, feeling very embarrassed and depressed, and tell us their life story and why they joined the party. It was the saddest experience to see these kind of people, in the clutches of their own despair, knowing it but feeling hopeless and unable to alter anything. They felt their only option was to be an obedient sheep. These people needed more help and careful attention than the others. They suffered all different kinds of depression in their lives, and a few of them had even attempted suicide. It was horrible to hear stories like that. More than anything else, these lost people needed to feel accepted by someone. Often even their own families would turn their backs on them, and their friends and coworkers were scared of them as Communists or disgusted by their party membership.

As the week at the camp progressed, people's faces would change and the environment of love and joy would penetrate their hearts. They felt differently in their health and fitness level, too, thanks to the daily exercises. It was truly a week of high physical and mental activity, which almost all of them were tasting for the first time in their lives. It was the most wonderful feeling for us who were creating the program—to see happiness and relaxing images around us.

An important and happy break came usually in the middle of the week, after an evening *satsang* in which we focused on joy. It was the fourth day of camp, and people would suddenly start talking to each other more openly. It seemed the day could not end without their sharing appreciation for the things they had experienced in the camp so far and joy at finding good friends around them. A mutual spirit of happiness prevailed among the group, and even those still in a doubtful mood would slowly let their general outlook turn into sunshine. It would be the day when someone would come up to me and ask me a question like, "Olga, do you think that there is God?" "Is there life after I die?" "Can I help my mother and father to be more happy?" "Can I do something around the camp to help out?" There was a sudden change and a need in their hearts to gain more knowledge about their lives, as well as developing a more serving spirit. We as camp organizers didn't have to ask for help in the kitchen anymore, or repeat the call for a cleaning committee. They would bring beautiful wild flowers from nearby woods to decorate the main hall and make it more inviting, or some of them with more creative talents would paint pictures or make small gifts for others. The bags which served as repositories for mutual expressions of our spiritual vitamins would suddenly be filled with notes to each other.

From this day until the end of a camp session, there were fewer sad, cloudy, dispirited, and blue faces and more flourishing, cheerful, and joyful ones. We actually put a sign—"House of Joy"—on the front door of the main camp building as a reminder that "in the cottage there is joy," as our Church hymn states. We sang the hymn "Love at Home" at camp, being careful not to identify the source of the song, and as we sang, tears flooded people's faces. You could easily say that many of them had never before experienced what they felt while singing this hymn for the first time in their lives.

On the last day of camp, many people were sad because they didn't want to leave. Especially sad were those who were stubborn in the beginning and yet later on witnessed great changes and saw that life could be different for them. However, it was often painful for them to go back to their pre-camp lives. They knew they would have to make some adjustments and changes and perhaps also felt that they would end up as sheep running away from the wolves. Because we knew we could expect this kind of reaction, we tried to build an optimistic spirit from the start of each camp session, and we were positive and encouraging to those who asked us, "May I write you at least once a month?" Some who later wrote expressed gratitude for changes in their lives, and some wrote for further advice. It was not unusual for a former participant to say something like "My family doesn't understand me. They thought that I had gone crazy when I started to talk to them about my feelings and experiences from the camp. I think I need some advice from you about how to deal with it a little bit better. Do you have any ideas?"

We gathered all the people together on the last evening of camp and organized something close to a testimony meeting. Each person had the opportunity to share what he or she had learned during the week. These moments were the most beautiful moments of the camp for me. To see tears on the face of a man who had declared earlier that he would never change his life's attitude, and then to see his beautiful shining smile and happiness during that last evening at camp, was amazing to me. Some cried at this meeting because of the new happiness they had found, and others because of the bitter reality that they had to make some important changes. During that meeting we heard comments like these:

"I have never witnessed so much love and joy in my life."

"I feel that I saved my life from suicide and my family from disaster."

"I will apologize to my brother with whom I haven't spoken for almost twenty years."

"I have quit smoking and drinking, thanks to your influence this week."

Sometimes participants approached us with serious questions for which they needed guidance before returning to their homes:

"Help me end my membership in the Communist party. Tell me how I can do it without hurting my career and my family."

"All you teach us here sounds practically unacceptable in my everyday life, because it is too positive and naive in today's world. However, I feel in my heart that it is somehow good. But very hard!"

"I have tried to get into the university six times, but I have never been accepted because my father was a political rebel in the Prague Spring of 1968. What are my chances in life?"

These were just a few of people's questions and cries. They desperately wanted specific advice, but it was very difficult to help them in many cases. There were no simple answers: people had to take many small steps, we knew, in order to overcome large problems. Some people understood this, and others felt discouraged and unable to change. Some folks even came back to the camp after their week was over, just to check in with us and get a little recharge. I witnessed many changes in people's lives during my ten years of working at the yoga camps.

One thing that kept us strong and united as camp workers was that all the Latter-day Saints participating in each camp would meet every evening for Book of Mormon study and a prayer. On the last night of each camp, we felt like a small army of God, able to do a small part of his work and much the happier for it. We knew that our freedom and actions had iron boundaries, and all our activities had the potential to be extremely dangerous and unsafe for our future. Each of us could easily have been thrown in prison for at least seven years, according to our Communist governmental laws, if the true purpose of our camp were known. But the Lord blessed and protected us, and we continued to try to bring a tiny portion of the light of the gospel into others' lives through our work at yoga camps. Although our own knowledge of the gospel and Church doctrines was in an infantile stage and very limited, we knew that Heavenly Father knew our circumstances and would forgive our lack of gospel scholarship and bless us for the unofficial preparatory missionary work we were doing. We prayed for and looked toward a day when things would be done differently, when the Church would exist publicly; but at that time it didn't, and we knew this was reality and weren't sad because of it. We believed our efforts would be successful in the long run as a preparation for missionary work at some future time when freedom would open its doors to our beloved Czechoslovakia.

I am sure that if any longtime member of the Church from the United States had come to these camps, he or she probably would not have understood our efforts, which mixed the physical good of cleansing the body and the physical benefits of hatha yoga exercises with the good of the gospel. If new arrivals in the Missionary Training Center in Provo had seen a video of the camp without any explanation, they would perhaps think that these Czech Saints were off the track. But I believe the Lord prepares his people and every land in his own way, according to the circumstances and the times in which the people live. We trusted that inspiration and opportunities came to us because the Lord wanted to prepare his people for the future.

These Czech Saints, young and old, who worked so hard to plant gospel seed in hard ground are heroes in my eyes. They didn't cast down their eyes in front of the Communists and didn't allow their spirits to be broken by danger or the fear which surrounded them every day.

The first two years, only Otakar and Gád Vojkůvka and myself worked as camp leaders. Our work was physically and mentally very exhausting for just the three of us. After five weeks and five consecutive camp sessions, I would come home and sleep for a couple of days to regain my energy.

However, I also felt like a new person because of the joy it brought me to be gaining appreciation for missionary work within the Church, even though there was no official, authorized way to serve a mission at that time in my country. Through yoga camps I realized how much people in my country thirsted for the gospel in their lives, yet they didn't believe in God and often many times laughed at the mere mention of his existence. However, when the right circumstances occurred, they listened to gospel principles— especially when those principles were introduced to them on the level and in language of their understanding. People were able to be touched by the Spirit of the Holy Ghost even though they didn't recognize what that influence was—just as I had been when I first entered Brother Vojkůvka's house.

10

THE SCHOOL OF WISDOM

The more camps we did, the more we realized that there had to be another way to keep in touch with some people from the camp who really wanted to continue their progress but didn't know how to do it on their own. We knew that we couldn't just invite all of the people to the Brno branch and introduce them directly to the Church. The next step occurred very naturally, and I felt it was an answer to our prayers.

"Could you come to my city and give a public lecture? I think that I could organize it. We have a lot of people from your yoga courses who would be interested in coming and bringing their families. What do you think?" one man asked in a letter which he wrote me a couple of months after a yoga camp.

I talked to Brother Vojkůvka because I didn't know how safe this kind of public activity would be. He thought it was a very good idea if it could be done in the right way. When I prayed about this activity, I felt it was right to accept these speaking engagements. Soon Brother Vojkůvka and I began presenting lectures in different corners of Czechoslovakia.

My life became busy and happy as never before. Usually participants from our yoga camps would organize these public lectures either in their workplaces, sport clubs, schools, or public cultural halls. It was not so hard for me to manage my school schedule to include this new activity, since I had adjusted well to the university school system after the few first shocks. Because my fellow students often socialized in a dancing club or a drinking bar, I did not spend much time with the student crowd in general. The difference between us was so visible that my fellow students eventually stopped bothering me to join their activities, and whenever they saw me busily running out of class after school they were confused and asked me, "Why are you so busy? Do you have so many boyfriends to take care of or what?"

To prepare for a public lecture was a harder task than I had imagined. I faced at least two groups of people: those who were genuinely interested in yoga and the critics, who included Communists and secret police. I would arrive in a city I didn't know too much about, and the only faces I recognized would be those I had gotten to know at a yoga camp, those who had asked me to come. Sometimes there would be thirty people at the lecture, other times two or three hundred. I would never have thought that I could give public lectures that incorporated some gospel principles and were presented to large audiences, but Heavenly Father protected me while doing this, even though a lot of secret police members attended these lectures quite regularly.

What could I share with my audiences? I wondered. I decided to focus on two main subjects: health and morality. They seemed to be neutral issues in the eyes of Communists, and yet for me they were a door through which I could hopefully offer a ray of light to my listeners. Health was always a hot topic, and moreover, yoga was commonly understood as a way to gain general health and was becoming popular in the country. Morality was a difficult but very good subject even from the Communist point of view. It was apparently obvious to even the Communists that people suffered a great deal from hating each other, lying, stealing, and lacking a general sensitivity for moral principles, so the topic of morality was more than safe—it was even highly appropriate—to discuss openly and publicly. People would shift uncomfortably in their chairs while I was introducing this subject; they wondered if I was going to start in with some kind of a Marxist-Leninist lecture about moral principles (meaning the great benefits of Communist philosophy). But in a few minutes they fell silent. The words I used were different from common Communist moral phrases, which were filled with hypocrisy. These words were understandable and reached directly to their hearts—which was entirely due to the fact that I was teaching gospel principles, and the gospel can naturally penetrate the human soul.

With both these topics I found out that I could easily open other related themes during our discussions. It was very hard work. The public halls didn't have one bit of an inviting spirit but were gloomy and cold. Not only would the policemen be sitting there together with the secret police in each corner of the room, but a certain portion of the audience sat and watched without any participation, there just to satisfy curiosity. To change such an atmosphere was as hard as bringing a smile to a child who has decided to scowl for the rest of an evening or like bringing sunshine to a worm-eaten pessimist who knows only sarcastic and ironic humor. To transform this icy spirit among the people to a warm and sharing one was to learn a new art.

Czech and Slovak young and middle-aged people who were educated in the Communist school system would always either accept the whole idea of one of my lectures or reject it. For them the real meat of thinking was a scientifically grounded reality of facts. They liked statistics from scientific research or connected to a certain scientist's name, and these facts would sometimes persuade them to agree to something new. Science was holy for Communists. It made them think that they could become rulers of universal forces, the world itself. Above all, they liked to hear any fact that would help them to convince all religious people that God did not exist. Even for people who didn't believe Communist philosophy, this "scientific" offshoot of Communist ideology influenced people's minds and became a very strong force for atheism in Czechoslovakia. It was sad to see people become adamant about some new scientific truth they had just read in a magazine or heard on TV, then connect this with any other morsels of science they thought they understood, and finally struggle to come up with a "universal truth" that was proven, in their minds, by these scattered "truths."

Recently I read, "That is one great difficulty with the philosophers of the world, as it now exists, that man claims himself to be the inventor of everything he discovers. Any new law and principle which he happens to discover he claims to himself instead of giving glory to God" (John Taylor, *The Gospel Kingdom,* sel. G. Homer Durham [Salt Lake City: Bookcraft, 1987], p. 47).

It was my personal observation from these first public encounters that I had to be very specific in order to make an acceptable point for a listening audience. However, my lessons weren't designed to persuade someone to believe in issues I was trying to introduce. Rather, I hoped to teach by the Spirit and be able to open people's hearts and minds. I introduced topics such as the importance of respecting ourselves as well as our fellowmen. To support these ideas I would retell a famous folk fable, share life experiences (my own or those of others), then finish with a strong statement by a person they could relate to and respect: a philosopher, a politician, a historian, etc.

I was helped in my member-missionary efforts in such strange and limiting circumstances by Brigham Young's declaration that "every true philosopher, so far as he understands the principles of truth, has so much of the Gospel, and so far, he is a Latter-day Saint, whether he knows it or not" (Brigham Young, *Discourses of Brigham Young,* comp. John A. Widtsoe [Salt Lake City: Deseret

Book Company, 1954], p. 2). I tried to follow the advice that Paul gave while teaching the gospel to his fellowmen: "For though I be free from all men, yet have I made myself servant unto all, that I might gain the more. And unto the Jews I became as a Jew, that I might gain the Jews; to them that are under the law, as under the law, that I might gain them that are under the law. . . . To the weak became I as weak, that I might gain the weak: I am made all things to all men, that I might by all means save some. And this I do for the gospel's sake, that I might be partaker thereof with you" (1 Cor. 9:19–23).

As a result of these public lectures, presented mainly by Brother Otakar Vojkůvka and myself in the beginning and later by a few other new young members of the Church, a number of new yoga classes were established, and we gradually gained opportunities to meet with people in their homes and in small discussion groups made up of people who became our good friends through the lectures and classes. Without the constraints of public meetings, we could be more open in our teachings when we felt the direction of the Spirit to do so.

When we began our member-missionary efforts, there were only a few small branches of the Church in Czechoslovakia: one in Prague, one in Plzeň, and one in Brno. There were other places and cities where Czech Saints lived, but apparently they didn't gather for meetings of any kind. The city of Brno became gradually a small unofficial missionary headquarters. In this city, the capital of Moravia, we (myself, Brother Otakar Vojkůvka, and other young converts) established an informal learning center where we coordinated our efforts for preparing the Czech people to receive the gospel eventually. We called Brother Otakar Vojkůvka's unofficial missionary training program the School of Wisdom, and we began meeting as a group in 1986 in the Vojkůvkas' house once a month in the beginning. Our idea gradually spread to other cities like Uherské Hradiště, Ostrava, Jihlava, Mladá Boleslav, Jičín,

Pardubice, Plzeň, and also in Trenčín and Bratislava, Slovakia. This was our way of unofficially preparing for the future establishment of real, conventionally organized missionary work. Our unofficial groups would later be replaced by officially organized branches of the Church after full-time missionaries entered the country in 1990.

In the School of Wisdom, we taught former yoga camp participants who were eager to continue associating with our newly baptized young members. In this smaller, more focused group, we could introduce these people to gospel principles and, after much preparation, to the Church. The steps had to be a very gradual path leading closer to Church doctrines each time we met together. The School of Wisdom was the first place where our yoga camp friends could hear us broach the topic of God's existence. Although many of the participants had known us for years before participating in the school, it was quite a shock for some of them to realize that we actually believed in God. For many of them this fact was a barrier, even a disappointment, when they heard it for the first time. We discussed with our listeners the disappointment of wrongly worshipping false gods that will disappoint them. We also tried to help people understand that the real art of living is to leave an old idea or belief and replace it with a higher one.

We felt that an important first step would be helping people see the need for changing their destructive behavior—in other words, the need for personal repentance. In the beginning we tried to speak about gospel principles, using gospel language directly from the New Testament. We soon realized that people could not understand and weren't able to relate to Christ, not even in a general sense. Religion was very new to them, and gospel terms still were hard spiritual meat to digest. The more experience we gained, the more we could see that we needed to first help them overcome their lack of direction and motivation. Their ideas about life and their future were so pessimistic that they didn't see any need to become better as individuals. Personal improvement made no sense to them. They generally saw virtue and morality as old-fashioned, unreal, and silly. This was not because they were intrinsically evil but because their Communist-influenced education had confused all the true principles of human life and had produced loneliness, a sense of inadequacy, and a general apathy.

Therefore, our teaching began, as in the yoga camps, with hatha yoga and other ancient yoga principles. We found that practicing hatha yoga exercises in conjunction with teaching some of yoga's moral principles helped participants to prepare to live with integrity and serve others. Our students needed to gain an understanding of self-respect and self-esteem in order to gain a personal testimony of the most basic elements of the gospel and to gain an understanding of the true meaning of love and service. Most of the participants from the School of Wisdom kept a personal journal in which they would set exact practical and ethical goals that they wanted to understand and use daily. These practices became stepping-stones between the students' final yoga training and their introduction into the gospel of Jesus Christ.

We introduced the gospel only to those people who understood and accepted the necessity of change and who sought true repentance and saw the need to be engaged in doing something good in their own lives. The challenge was helping students reach that point. It was sad to witness just how much Communism had destroyed family life and had replaced it with mutual intolerance and hate among family members. This had caused so much pain in these young people's lives. Other issues such as smoking, drinking, bad friends, etc., were also problems for them, but the family issue was the most challenging one. Because Communist leaders insisted on civic and public activity at the expense of family life, many of our young students seemed lost in their own selfishness. At first they did not view their state as a problem. Their parents either didn't mean anything to them or just were a source of constant friction.

Brother Vojkůvka was especially skilled in helping individuals to find a way to resolve their problems in these areas of recognition of the need for, and motivation for, personal change. Some of them were so slow to believe and spent hours with this good man, receiving wise counsel from him. But if a family or relationship problem was resolved and a person understood that certain changes had to be made, usually true repentance was not far behind.

I have to mention that ninety-nine percent of all these young people would have had no support at home if they had mentioned one word about God. I knew a number of young people whose parents found out about their son or daughter's religious activity and immediately threw them out of the house. It was a miracle when someone brought their parents to Church meetings. The rare older people who were baptized became not only pioneers in the gospel but also heroes to all members because of the great uphill path they had climbed to membership in the Church.

We Latter-day Saints felt such joy when we saw that people attending our discussions were growing in the general principles of faith. Good moral principles gradually gave them a strong testimony of what great differences—even miracles—can happen when a person is engaged in good things. This faith slowly grew to believing in Jesus Christ as Savior and accepting his atonement.

It was the most beautiful thing to see baptisms of young people who took the gospel and their Church membership very seriously into their hearts. It was great to witness the miracle of positive change in people's lives. The restored gospel and the personal testimony which they obtained meant not only a new way of looking at life but also the new sensation of living in the sun after many years of darkness. When young new members came to the Sunday meetings, their presence brightened our congregation like sunlight pouring through a large window that had been shuttered for years. First of all, newly baptized members—both young and old—were able to build a bridge of great communication and love with each other and with branch members in a short period of time. Every new person was especially welcomed with hugs, tears of joy, and expressions of mutual understanding. Now, more than ever, I could see why the longtime Czech members were so gracious and so radiant with happiness in the spirit when they welcomed new members into the Church. These events brought a renewed joy into their hearts as they saw a long-expected hope come true, although they had waited until their heads were gray with years before witnessing the miracles of Church growth. We were one family, and for some members, the Church family was the only one they had.

One of the challenges we faced in the Church with newly baptized members was the fact that they were fundamentally unfamiliar with the scriptures. In the beginning of our member-missionary efforts in the 1980s, only a few copies of the Book of Mormon were available among the members. The new converts were of course thirsty to read this "most perfect of any scripture," and many copied pages of their favorite passages from the few copies rotated among the members. We did not have a copy of the Doctrine and Covenants or the Pearl of Great Price. It was quite a challenge for converts to learn about the living prophet, Ezra Taft Benson. We didn't hear or read any of his messages from the general conference because it wasn't possible to receive any videocassettes or copies of the *Ensign*. Therefore, when we learned of the prophet's inspired directive to read the Book of Mormon, we couldn't fully comprehend it. We supposed that it has *always* been important to read scriptures. Many new members asked me, "Why wouldn't a member read the Book of Mormon?" Many times I pondered their statements and thought how wonderful it would be to know the whole context of the prophet's inspiration about reading the Book of Mormon and why was it so significant at the time for members.

At that time it was hard to understand the prophet's message out of context, but little did I know that in 1990 I would have the privilege of personally visiting the October general conference. It was a dream come true but also a feast hard to wholly digest. I spoke almost no English at that time, but the language of love I witnessed was strong enough to penetrate my entire soul. I was amazed to feel the Spirit radiating through our living apostles and other servants of the Lord who spoke at that time. I had only one wish: that the Czech members could feel and see the same as I could, and then they would understand without words the importance of the new messages which were delivered to all the Saints all over the world at that time. I received a personal inspiration from all that I heard and felt at the conference, and I especially gained a love for obedience to God's law.

The very first contact I had with a Church representative from Western Europe was with the president of the Austria Vienna Mission, Ed Morrell, and his wife, Norma Toronto Morrell.

"Dobrý den, sestro!" Brother Morrell said in greeting me. It means "Good day, sister!" Brother Morrell spoke Czech! It was unbelievable to me that an American would actually try to learn a language which only nine million people speak in the whole world! I learned he had been a missionary in Czechoslovakia in the 1930s, when the Czech mission was first established. It was quite an event for all the members to meet him and his wonderful wife. Most of the older members knew him, and I could see through their faces what it must have been like to have a real mission in Czechoslovakia many years ago. Suddenly new waves of life came to their hearts, and all the years of persecution became invisible and unimportant in the face of the fact that they were now reunited with someone who was a part of happier times and who had helped lay the foundation of the Church in our country.

I was impressed with both the Morrells. Occasionally, I would see an American on a street as a tourist, but I had never had the chance to talk to any of them. The Morrells were the very first Americans I could talk to, face to face. Just their presence brought us hope and the important connection which the Church members had been deprived of for dozens of years. What was more exciting was that in the coming years, their visits became more regular (well, at least from our perspective); they visited once or twice a year. After they finished their mission in Austria, we had a chance to meet with the regional representative for Europe, Brother Johann Wondra, and his wife, Ursula, both from Vienna, Austria. What extraordinary, exemplary, and faithful people! We felt that our missionary efforts in the Church in Czechoslovakia had at last been recognized outside our country.

We needed more copies of the Book of Mormon for newly baptized members. Our special desire was that these copies be printed in a small format so that one could hide them in a pocket or under an arm while in public and not have them recognized at first glance by strangers as religious scriptures. How grateful we were when we saw the first copies in our hands, printed to a size of 3.5 by 5.5 inches! It was just the perfect format, even down to the dark maroon cover with the outer edge in bright red, which made the book look almost like a Communist handbook. No one on the subway would ever guess that we were toting around the most precious scripture. It was perfect for our missionary needs at that time! In the beginning it was two courageous men, Brothers Morrell and Wondra, who always brought a few copies hidden in their suits and coat pockets. It was a dangerous stunt to bring a whole packet, since the Czech police would surmise that there was a certain necessity for the book within the country.

I remember particularly one episode at the Czech-Austrian border that happened to Brother Wondra. In spring 1988, Brother Wondra was traveling to a small local Church conference in Brno. This time he took more copies of the Book of Mormon than usual. Czech customs officers looked in this car and found in a suitcase in his trunk some copies of the Book of Mormon in English, German, Polish, and Czech.

They shook their heads, talked to each other, and then came to him and asked, "Why do you have so many copies of this book?"

"Because I love it" was his short reply.

The Czech customs officers weren't angry but did send him back to Austria just the same, telling him that he could enter the country, but only without "those books." He did return to Vienna, arriving the same day to the conference without the books. Although the Czech-Austrian borders were always sharply watched by the Czech border police, this was a very light punishment that Brother Wondra received. If the same episode had happened only a few years earlier, before Gorbachev came onto the political scene in Eastern European politics, the Czech police wouldn't ever have allowed Brother Wondra to cross the Czech borders again.

We greatly benefited from any visit of the Morrells and Wondras. It was great to see some of their children. Especially for our young members, it was a great testimony to see foreign young members among us and to get at least a hint of the worldwide nature of the Church. There were other American members of the Church who would come to visit occasionally. One was Ed Strobel from Idaho, who miraculously always brought some Church books, tapes, pictures, etc. He was literally like Santa Claus whenever he came, as we would be enriched with new Church materials which we lacked so severely. I don't have a clue as to how he could bring so many materials. Tom Hrncirik from California, who traveled to Czechoslovakia to find his ancestors in Moravia, brought us more smiles, encouragement, and even more understanding in the gospel ordinances. Once he visited our small branch in Uherské Hradiště. He had to leave right after the sacrament meeting, and I was the one who accompanied him to the front door to say good-bye.

"Olga, there shouldn't be a hymn played on the tape recorder during the time of partaking the sacrament," he smiled and gently whispered.

"Thanks a lot," I replied and shared the idea with the priesthood holders afterwards. Since that Sunday we have followed Brother Hrncirik's advice.

Starting in the late 1980s, we even met a few General Authorities, although the Communist government still dominated my country. These great leaders, though they had only a few hours' layover between their flights, had prearranged a small meeting with the Saints in Prague. I remember Elder Joseph B. Wirthlin of the Quorum of the Twelve, along with Elder Carlos E. Asay, a member of the Presidency of the Seventy, visiting us one afternoon. They held a small meeting with the young people in Brother Šnederfler's home in Prague. The Czech young members were very open and asked a lot of questions. It was a great experience for me to see the steadfastness and pure love of Christ these two men possessed. I thought more about these men, and from that day on, they became my personal examples.

Sister Barbara Winder, the Relief Society general president at that time, also visited us with her husband, Richard. I was the Relief Society president of Brno branch at that time, and I had the privilege of spending a few moments with Sister Winder. I was so amazed at the beautiful, positive, ever-smiling, and encouraging spirit she radiated. I didn't speak any English, so our conversation was limited, but I don't recall getting any more hugs from someone in a shorter period of time than we had from Sister Winder. She was amazing. Her visit meant a great deal to me, since I had been called as a Relief Society president but didn't have a clue as to what I was doing.

A great highlight of those years was President Thomas S. Monson's visit to Czechoslovakia just a few years before the great changes took place in my country and Eastern Europe. He also came just for one afternoon during his layover at the Prague airport. I was amazed by his energy, his great smile, and his warm, familiar approach with all of us who attended the meeting that day. He encouraged us to be faithful and said that we had to become ready for the Church's being reopened in Czechoslovakia in the future. We listened in astonishment to these prophetic words and believed him completely. In particular, President Monson counseled us to read and study the scriptures and come to understand the Book of Mormon, even the difficult passages in it. I was surprised to hear this, because it was an echo of counsel given in my patriarchal blessing, which I had received from Austrian Patriarch Rupert Fuchshofer on June 8, 1986, in Brno. I knew President Monson's words were inspired, and I started reading the Book of Mormon with more diligence from that day on.

11

MIRACLES OF CONVERSION
IN MY FAMILY

While managing and organizing summer yoga camps, I thought about my parents all the time. How wonderful it would be to have them there and to see their lives lighten up as they came in contact with the restored gospel! I prayed constantly from the day of my own baptism to be an instrument in the Lord's hands in their conversion. There was nothing more important to me. They were great parents, and I knew that they wouldn't have to make major adjustments to be ready for baptism. They lived the Word of Wisdom already, and their lives, based on principles of charity and moral integrity, were always exemplary to the rest of my family. The more I thought about them, the more I longed to have the right opportunity to tell them the good news of the gospel of Jesus Christ.

The ground needed to be prepared carefully. Religious thoughts or topics certainly weren't a common part of our family discussions. The beast of Communism had cast its shadow on our family too, and we didn't openly discuss God. The Church wasn't recognized publicly, and Latter-day Saints were persecuted. Above all, there wasn't a branch in my hometown. I was the only member of the Church there. These are a few of the issues that made it a challenge for me to be a good missionary to them. When I look back on my high school days, I can see that I was a hungry, searching teenager who wanted to ask questions on a sensitive topic but didn't have enough courage to take the first step. There is a Czech expression "Chodila jako kočka kolem horké kaše"—she was walking like a cat around a hot pot—that described me exactly.

Headaches! They are painful and nobody likes them, but I am grateful for them because this common malady turned out to be the key to a great missionary tool that worked for me many times. Because of the help of a secretary at the sport club who suffered bad headaches, I had opened my first yoga classes, which had opened the door to many people who had embraced the gospel.

My mom suffered not only headaches but severe migraines in her late fifties. She knew nothing about yoga, and I didn't really think it could help her all that much. However, it was painful to watch how much she suffered, lying on the sofa with a cold towel around her head. The whole family engine stopped, and we felt lost and helpless as we walked quietly around her and changed one cool towel for another. I began to study as much literature as I could find that might shed some light on the nature of headaches.

"Mom, I want to teach you how to relax and strengthen some muscles in your neck. It might help you," I said to her one Friday night in 1983.

"Well, you know that I always trust you," she said. In a few minutes we were sitting together and my dad joined us. I demonstrated a few very simple exercises and a basic relaxation method.

"I'll do these exercises with you whenever I'm at home, but you have to promise me that you will also do them every day on your own," I said.

She agreed to do so, and within a few months she not only got rid of her headaches but also became interested in yoga. I actually could hardly believe it when she told me one day that her headaches were gone. "None of the pills had helped me, but those exercises did the trick. I think your father and I will enroll in your yoga classes next session."

I was so happy. I gave her a big bear hug and felt like I had won an Olympic gold medal. Later she always recalled this first "headache experience" as a great opening testimony for her to start a new path of her life. This led first to yoga classes and later on to joining The Church of Jesus Christ of Latter-day Saints.

My dad was always conservative towards new thoughts but also sensitive enough to figure out when something good or bad was happening to me, all without saying one word. He, as well as my mom, could see that certain changes had occurred in my life. I was smiling more, I was very happy, and—miracle of all miracles—even the books in my room ended up more often in their proper place in the shelf! They saw that I was spending a lot of time studying scriptures and other religious books. Many people would come over every weekend to visit me, seeking some kind of encouragement or even advice. Most of these people were those who participated in yoga camps and yoga sessions in my hometown and needed to be cheered up or just to come to chat a few minutes about some topic which had stuck in their minds.

This parade was a new phenomenon, and my parents realized that I was involved in something new and unusual. However, because they both took my yoga classes, they knew some of the people and assumed that I was trying, as my visitors' yoga teacher, to help them to release their physical pain and overcome physical stress and health problems.

I invited my parents to come to a yoga camp the summer after their first year of yoga practice. To my delight, they came and were willing to sacrifice a week of their vacation to do so! It was wonderful to see them exercising, eating the unusual wheat diet (not too enjoyable for either one of them), observing, and listening to all the lectures. I watched their reactions carefully. I assumed that my dad would be more conservative and would keep a distance from the whole program. I was totally wrong. He loved the entire program and within a few days was fully immersed in it. I almost saw myself while watching his reactions to the first serious topic. I was secretly grinning whenever I looked at his smiling, happy face. He talked to other yoga participants and made many friends that week, which was amazing to me.

My mom was the one who had to make a few more adjustments, to my surprise. She was very confused when she saw people crying while sharing their life stories. She didn't feel comfortable with people's openness, so unlike the usual pattern of life in Communist Czechoslovakia, and she didn't think all that sharing of feelings and emotions was really necessary. But within a few days I had a chance to talk to her. She opened her heart and shared with me some of the difficult experiences of her childhood, and we felt a new bond of increased understanding growing between us.

Both of my parents joined the Church very shortly after their first yoga camp experience. I had the privilege, together with Brother Holcman, to prepare them for their baptism. They loved the Book of Mormon from the beginning. I was amazed to see how spiritually mature they were, how prepared and open they were to the gospel, more than I had ever realized they would be. They both separately received very personal revelations that Joseph Smith was a true prophet, more quickly than I had, actually. For them, each doctrine was like picking a ripe fruit from a tree! They were ready to partake of the fruit; they just needed to know where the tree was. It told me a lot about their wonderful and humble hearts. To hear their testimony from their hearts for the first time in my life was as sweet as anything I have ever experienced. These wonderful Saints were my parents! Their testimonies illuminated even more my very own. It was as if we had finally met after a long journey, or after having been lost from each other for a long time. We knew that from that time forward, we wouldn't be lost ever again.

On July 23, 1985, their baptism took place in the same

location as my own, and also late in the evening. It was still in the dark days of Communism. My mother shared with me later her unique experience: "I felt like I was going to my own funeral. I was even humming an old Catholic funeral hymn, although I had been a Protestant all my life." But the baptism occurred without incident, and the Lord protected us as these sacred ordinances were performed. Afterwards we smiled and hugged. I knew how sincere and humble they both were regarding the covenants they accepted with their baptism. They both experienced the true meaning of baptism as "an end and a new beginning" in their lives. None of us knew how this wonderful experience would change our lives forever!

After their baptism, the three of us sat at the kitchen table holding hands, and the tears of happiness just wouldn't stop. Since my parents' baptism, tears of happiness have filled our house very often.

"This calls for a celebration!" my mom said, "and we should make Oli's favorite 'bomb toast' for all three of us."

"Wow, you must love me a lot!" I responded, and we laughed together. Bomb toast is a wacky combination of ingredients. I was in love with ketchup at the time I invented it. Especially in the winter months, as when this occasion took place, there weren't a lot of fresh fruits or vegetables available in my country. So in the winter, after a demanding marathon of five hours of yoga classes on Friday, I would come home and make my "bomb toast" to protect myself from the flu viruses. I would toast a piece of sour-dough bread until it was charred and almost black, then spread on ketchup, then add hard cheese, mustard, a few pickles, and a couple of cloves of cut garlic. Needless to say, I recommend this snack only for adventurous souls and special life situations! The simple food was great, somehow just right on this special evening as we first shared family testimonies about Joseph Smith and the restored gospel.

"Great beginnings happen within small walls!" my dad said,

smiling as all three of us sat around the kitchen table. This very same table was later to be of historical significance as it was the place where a new, small branch of the Church was established in my hometown just fourteen months later. At this very same table, in October 1986, my father was asked if he could accept the calling as branch president. I felt so proud and happy for him. It was a privilege to have my father as a faithful priesthood holder at home. My home felt so secure, homey, and truly heavenly to me—something I had never felt before, at least not to that extent!

One day I saw a painting depicting the very day when The Church of Latter-day Saints was organized in Joseph Smith's time. I realized that that event also took place in a tiny room! While I was looking at this illustration of an important Church event, my father's comment that "great beginnings happen within small walls" came to my mind again. I thought, Indeed, they do.

Our home literally became an open house for many young members and other new converts from my hometown, who had little or no support from their families. It is significant that many of these members call my parents "Dad" and "Mom"—even today. After my parents' baptism, it was rare that there would be only three of us at the dinner table. For most of the newly baptized members who constantly visited us, our small apartment became a future dream for their own families and homes.

"We came to feel the Spirit in your home and to rest for a minute to regain the strength to return to our parents," they would usually say. My parents would always understand.

It was quite a new experience for my dad, who had never conducted anything even remotely close to a church meeting in his life, to speak in front of the members as the very first branch president in my hometown of Uherské Hradiště. Everybody loved him for his humble heart, great sense of responsibility, dignity, and love which he put into the preparation of every Sunday meeting in our small apartment on the third floor. I came home on Fridays and would always see my dad studying the scriptures in his office, making notes and preparing himself to conduct the meetings or to give a talk. In the beginning, he was nervous as a new branch president. He had never seen an LDS church meeting conducted before and didn't want to do anything wrong. He was always excited to read me the talk he had prepared during the week and would always ask me what I thought. His thoughts were always right to the point of the gospel, without any of the unnecessary detours that new members were sometimes inclined to include (including myself).

"I don't want to embarrass the Lord and his marvelous work. He knows that I am a beginner and weak, but that doesn't mean that I have to make too many mistakes," he would explain.

It was marvelous to me to see how the gospel brought out more vividly and in more spiritual depth what wonderful and precious souls my parents have always been! They have become exemplary members to me as I have seen how much pure love they have for the Savior. It's great to see them in the service of the Lord! The best gift I could possibly have received from our Heavenly Father was certainly to see my very own parents illuminated by the gospel. What a miracle it was and still is to me! Their goodness was enriched and enhanced. Their Christlike love, which has always been rooted in their hearts, even when they didn't identify it as such, could suddenly flow freely and without any hesitation, a hug needing no special occasion as an excuse.

Actually, hugging became a significant change of behavior in our new Latter-day Saint family lifestyle. Thanks to learning new gospel principles every day, we all were able to express how much we loved each other more freely and openly. There isn't anything more sweet in my family than to receive the firm and assuring hugs of love from each other that have been shared freely ever since the days of our baptisms! Before our gospel commitments, we knew we loved each other, but it was almost like a tradition in my country to express it only on special occasions, with very little emotion and even that, of brief duration. (The Russian tradition of hugging and kissing on the cheek, which came with the Communism and could be seen daily on TV among the Russian and Czech Communist leaders, strongly influenced negatively against the fraternal hug.) Now we feel such joy that we sometimes have to "hug in air" as we lift each other off the ground with our vigorous hugs. The gospel has healed all the hard times and life challenges we have faced, together or as individuals, in those strange Communist times.

I have yet to see all my family and extended family join the Church. Some of our family expressed concern and even anger when they learned of the baptisms of my mom, my dad, and me. However, one of my brothers, Zdeněk, joined the Church several years after my parents, and we continue to pray that more miracles will take place.

Several years after my parents' baptism, I had the opportunity to briefly bear testimony of one aspect of the gospel when my father's oldest brother, Josef, died. He was in his early sixties at the time. I attended my uncle's funeral and visited grieving Aunt Lilka afterward. We had not been close to Josef and Lilka for some years, so it took all my courage to knock on her door and enter her home.

"I have heard people speak highly of your yoga classes," Aunt Lilka said after a few moments of awkward silence.

"Well, I really enjoy teaching it," I said.

"How did you come to such a unique hobby?"

"Because I was searching for something meaningful in my life." I didn't know how she would take my answer.

"Did you find it?" Aunt Lilka said with surprise as she looked straight into my eyes.

"Yes, I did find it, and more than that. Can I help you somehow?" I asked.

"I don't know." She was exhausted, so I helped her lie down on the sofa. She rested for a while, then sat up and started crying. I sat next to her, embraced her with one arm, and held her hand. I don't know how much time passed as we sat that way, but when she stopped crying and calmed down, I felt the Spirit so strongly. I looked into her eyes and told her, "I know that this life doesn't end with death but it continues. I want to help you to meet your Josef again one day."

The Spirit was so strong that I saw a sudden smile on my aunt's tear-stained face. It was like a small star twinkling in the middle of a dark sky as the spark of the Spirit touched her. With my whole heart I knew she would join the Church. She did, a year later, and also became one of the great yoga teachers in my hometown and has taught and continued the yoga tradition even until today. She is also serving as first counselor in the Relief Society presidency of the Uherské Hradiště Branch.

While often visiting Aunt Lilka, I had an opportunity to speak to my cousin Josef. At first he wasn't excited either about yoga or the Church. However, later on he started dating a girl who had been taking my yoga classes for a couple of years. It was a great surprise to me to find him in one of my yoga classes with his girlfriend. We became close friends, and I was happy to have the privilege of teaching them six discussions before their baptisms. Within a couple of years of their baptisms, they were married in the Freiberg Temple. Josef is presently serving as first counselor in the Uherské Hradiště branch presidency. Josef and his wife struggled for a couple of years after their marriage to have a baby, and through Aunt Lilka's help, their names were placed on the Salt Lake Temple's prayer roll. Within one year they were rejoicing with their newborn son, Josef III.

The Lord works in marvelous ways. I feel so blessed that my parents, one of my brothers, Aunt Lilka, and cousin Josef and his wife joined the Church. What a beautiful opportunity I had with my parents to receive together with them a patriarchal blessing. When the Freiberg Temple was opened, I rejoiced with them as we received our own endowments. I would never have thought that I might have the unique privilege of witnessing the sealing of my parents for time and all eternity. It was one of the happiest moments of our lives to be sealed together as a family. God's love penetrated through our souls, and the three of us were crying as we knelt in the temple sealing room together.

The hardest work is in your own family! Certain challenges have remained constant in ours. It is hard to be a pioneer. There is so much to be done for my own family. All of those who have become members have been carefully watched by other family members. Whenever one of us makes a small mistake, it turns into "water in the mill" and we are sharply criticized. "Ah, so this is what Mormons are like!" they would sometimes comment. But as the years go by, other family members have had more and more opportunities to see the blessings the gospel has brought to our lives. It is interesting to me to see how these good moments usually bring silence and a meaningful pondering in someone's heart.

12

GRILLED BY THE
SECRET POLICE

I was sitting with a few new friends at the yoga camp on a sunny August afternoon when the mailman delivered a notice from my hometown police. It said that I must come to the police station the next day.

This came as quite a surprise to me, I had an uneasy feeling. I knew what they might want—information about Alena.

Alena was my best friend, the very next person to join the Church in Brno after my own baptism. We were so close that we knew practically everything about each other's life. Just a few days before I was summoned by the police, Alena had traveled from Czechoslovakia to Yugoslavia. Her official travel plans stated that she was staying in Yugoslavia for a couple of days with her daughter Nicole and another member of the Church, then returning to our country. But actually, she was trying to get into Austria, where she would apply for refugee status. This was a process we Czechs always called "escaping." Not defecting—that would be too political a word for it. It was always referred to as escaping. I was completely aware of Alena's plans in Yugoslavia. I knew she didn't plan to come back to Czechoslovakia.

Alena was not my only close friend at that time. I also had a boyfriend, a young man to whom I was engaged to be married. I'll call him Honza, though that is not his real name. Honza was a university student and also a recent convert to the Church. He and I had talked seriously about using the very same plan of escape as Alena. We intended to meet Alena and her daughter in Yugoslavia and go together to Austria.

When the orders from the police arrived, I knew something had gone wrong. Very wrong. I took my bags and was about to leave the camp when Honza came to me and told me that the police had stopped him in the elevator at his home and persuaded him to give them his passport, which he did. I was sure that the police were going to question me about leaving the country. I wondered how the police could have possibly learned our plans.

"Sit down please," I was told by a policeman when I entered a tiny room containing only two chairs, a small table, a few cabinets, and a large window. He pushed a button on a tape recorder under his table and began recording the whole discussion.

"Well, you know why you were invited to our office, don't you?" he started.

"No, I don't know," I replied shortly, and suddenly millions of other possibilities were running through my mind. What if it was because of my yoga camps, my lectures and traveling, or even my Church membership? We Czech Latter-day Saints were translating some Church materials, making our own copies, teaching people about the Church, baptizing—and all these activities were taboo in my country.

"Miss Kovářová, we know that you are a very smart and well-educated person, so you don't have to play any silly games with us."

"Please, would you be a little bit more specific? I don't know what you are talking about." I knew I would have to stay calm and be brief in my answers.

"You want to travel to Yugoslavia this summer, eh?" he suddenly started in.

"Well, yes," I answered.

"What is the purpose of your trip?"

"A vacation."

"Are you sure?"

"Yes, I am."

"Well, we have a little bit different information," he paused waiting for my reply. I sat and looked at him.

"We learned that you want to escape the country with your friend."

"I don't know anything about it," I said, stalling for time. I hoped to learn more about the source of the police's information.

"Well, well, you don't but we do. Give me your passport."

"I didn't bring it with me."

"You must bring it to our office today. One of the officers will drive you home and bring you and your passport back to our office."

"Why do you need my passport?"

"We will tell you when you get back. Thank you, and I hope to see you within one hour." He stood up, opening the door to let me know that it was the end of our first discussion.

I was guarded as I drove home; I could plainly see the unmarked police car following a short distance behind. I parked by the apartment building and walked inside. The man in the dark red car stayed in his car.

"I am in deep trouble. They are questioning me about the Yugoslavia trip," I whispered to my father.

I was trying to remember the words of Brother Otakar Vojkůvka, who was questioned many times by the police. His advice was always "They don't know anything unless you give them new information."

I felt hopeless and frightened. "But how did they find out? Who told them?" I desperately asked my father.

"Olga, it isn't important at this moment. Someone did. But

now you have to be focused to get out of this mess—that's your main goal," he said. My parents prayed together with me, my dad gave me a blessing, and I left the house. The red car was waiting with its engine on, and the man didn't mind that I realized he was watching my every move. It felt terrible to be under such scrutiny. This was very first time in my life when I was under the police microscope, and I didn't know where all this would lead. I returned to the police station, and this time I was told to speak with the head police officer at the passport department.

"You must be Miss Kovářová." He shook my hand and asked, "What bad thing is happening to you?"

"I don't really know. I had to go home and come back with my passport."

"That's very bad news."

"Why do you think so?"

"Because we need to take it from you and unfortunately you cannot travel to Yugoslavia."

"Why is that?"

"Well, this is our question for you, not your question for us," he said.

"I am sorry but I don't understand you."

"Do you know that when we assemble enough reasonable facts regarding your attempt to escape the country, you could be in prison from three to seven years? If you confess, you might not even go to court," he told me while carefully watching every move-ment of my eyes and my body.

"I am sorry but I don't think I should be threatened to confess to something which doesn't exist."

"Miss Kovářová, we have this paper, which tells us every detail about your plans," he said, waving a paper in his hand.

"Can I see it?"

"Do you think that we are so naive as to give it to you?"

"How should I respond?"

"Do you know what? We will give you another day to think about it. Let's stop this discussion now, and you can come to my office tomorrow at nine in the morning."

"I won't have anything new to tell you tomorrow."

"Well, we shall see."

I drove home but didn't see a car following me. Interesting, I thought. As soon as I got home, my mom told me to come and look out the bedroom window. We could see the same type of car as the red one that had followed me that morning.

"There are two men who have been watching our apartment with a telescope," she said.

"Mom, I must go back tomorrow," I said. "Someone must have told the police everything. They got a paper from someone who told them all about our summer plans."

Suddenly the doorbell rang and my boyfriend Honza was standing in the doorway.

"I am sorry. All this happened because of my mistake," he said. "I told my mom about our summer plans, and she went for advice to her police friend and told him that you were the one who actually planned everything. She didn't realize what kind of danger she caused to both of us." He said it all in one breath.

"I need to know exactly how much they know. Did you have a chance to talk to your mom and find out what she said to her police friend?"

"You know she doesn't like you at all," he said. "When I asked her what she told them, she said she didn't care. I couldn't find out anything. She is mad at me and hopes this will end our relationship."

I knew how much Honza's mother had disliked me when she found out about my membership in the Church, and especially when Honza and his older sister joined the Church. When Honza and I had begun discussing plans for marriage, his mother had made it very clear that I, with my foolish religious ideas, was not a good influence on her son.

As my boyfriend and I stood at the apartment door, I could sense he was wavering, irresolute. "How can I help you? What should I do?" he asked me.

"I am terrified and I am lying to them from the first moment," I said. "It is really hard. I don't know how much I can take."

"What are they asking you?"

"They are trying to figure out if all this is true. They were already threatening me with prison."

Honza said he would go home and talk to his mother; then he left. Although I was tired and scared, my parents were courageous and didn't show a bit of hopelessness or danger. "I know that you will be all right," my mom told me. "I have been praying for you, and I know that you will be protected."

I returned to the police office each day for the next four days. They took my passport, telling me that I would not even be allowed to travel to the Soviet Union! How ridiculous! I didn't have a bit of desire to do so anyway. On each of the next four days, I was questioned by a group of policemen instead of just one. Each time they brought me to the office of the head officer at the police station. They would be nice and polite to me one moment, offering coffee or cigarettes, even their own cloth napkins, and then so persuasive, with strict and terrifying words, the next moment as they tried to get me to confess what they wanted to hear. But I was always safe as long as I reminded myself that these were just words—scary words conjured up to strike fear in me.

I did not budge from my original story, nor did I say anything to myself in my mind to create self-doubts. I remained adamant, although they called other friends and school people to find out more details about my plans and activities. I was very fortunate in the end. The head officer asked me the very last question, which I will never forget: "Did you know that we got all this information from your future mother-in-law?"

Honza's mother was the informer! The officer looked at me, smiling and waiting for my reaction. I tried to make my face expressionless. The officer continued, "She was the one who gave the information to the police in her hometown, and that was how we found out about you." Then, almost with pride and self-satisfaction, he added, "We found out from her local police department just how much she hates you, and we found it a strong enough argument to think that she might be lying to us. She is your savage. Go home."

I couldn't believe that it ended up so peacefully yet so bitterly for me! Could the police really have chalked it up as a sour family affair in the end? I didn't understand and never found out why I was so fortunate and blessed that they let me go without any punishment. No car followed me when I left the office. I thought perhaps it was a new strategy on their part, but that was truly the end of their questioning.

I came out of this trouble with only one small scratch: although I got my passport back, the police informed me that authorities would never allow me to travel abroad in the future, except to Communist countries in Europe. They granted that I could travel even to Russia—but of course I had no desire to ever travel to the very center of Communist power.

As I returned from the last visit to the police station, I pondered the whole experience. I couldn't fathom how someone's hatred of the gospel and, because of that, even of me had actually saved me in this frightening and horrible experience. I knew I had to have a serious talk with Honza and that I couldn't marry someone unless I was certain of his unwavering commitment, both to me and to the gospel. In addition to that, I felt something really imperative had happened in my life. I felt like someone had changed the direction of my walking path, and being free from police surveillance was like walking from night into day.

My parents were so happy to see me back and to know that I didn't have to go back to the station again. Now I could see on their faces how worried they had been all through my trouble with the police. My mom had been especially worried, because I hadn't been able to eat for the past four days. I had lost almost ten pounds.

While resting in my bed that evening, I felt the Spirit strongly. The impression came to me, through the Spirit, that I should peacefully continue in my relationship with Honza but also keep my eyes open and observe. I was reassured that I had taken the right path in our relationship by bringing my friend to his baptism. The impression then came to me that Honza would need to find his own faith. I felt impressed to be patient: if any change was to occur in our relationship, I should wait for him to initiate it.

Afterwards I wasn't certain I had clearly understood the promptings of the Spirit, but I thought I had felt a distinct sense of warning. I wondered if the Lord was gently guiding me and preparing me for future events.

Honza came to visit me within a few days. He was different—nervous, distraught, like someone sitting on needles. He looked lost. We talked, and he told me that his parents had told him to decide between me and them. He said he didn't know what to do and asked that I give him some time.

I was unhappy and disappointed, and I cried many nights. But as more time passed, it became clear to me that Honza was swimming between both worlds—his family with their disdain for religion, and me and my family with our solid commitment to the Church. We both were trying our best, but there was a feeling of distance and sudden emptiness in our relationship. We remained good friends, and I remained somewhat uncertain about our future together.

About a year later, we went as a group of Czech Saints to the Freiberg Temple in East Germany. When we were leaving the temple, I saw my boyfriend's face and finally knew that our relationship was over. We returned to Czechoslovakia, and the next day Honza and I were sitting by a creek. There was silence. I knew what would happen. The Spirit had witnessed to me that the end of our relationship would be declared.

"It doesn't make any sense to continue this relationship," he said. He shook my hand and we wished each other a happy life. I had been prepared for this moment, but it still took a long time, even a few years, for the wound to heal. I wasn't happy when I saw that he missed Church more and more often on Sunday and eventually dropped into inactivity. I would visit him occasionally just to see how he was doing. Our lives and paths went in different directions. He remained a good man in his own way, however.

From these experiences I have learned that many times, despite hardship, great disappointment, or even personal danger, our Heavenly Father guides us on his own path if we are able to stay faithful and humble. I didn't understand for almost ten years why this all happened to me—wasn't I trying to do something good in the first place? However, one day, because of new events in my life, I came to the understanding that out of the messiness of it all, I could see that Heavenly Father had protected me and had given me other, greater blessings. But at the time of these experiences, I must admit that I saw no connection to any spirituality or growth of any kind. Today, I am happy to say that I am deeply grateful that these events changed my personal path of life.

I was questioned by the police on a few other occasions. They were always curious as to why my yoga activities were meeting with such success, but they never found out the real answer. It was an uneasy experience each time I went to the police station to face questions about my life and activities from all possible angles. Fortunately, I must say that I always came out without any harm or consequences. I felt protected because I knew that Heavenly Father cared for my soul and for my future.

13

A Little Communist Organization

The bitter experiences with the police and with my breakup with my boyfriend during summer 1985 changed a lot of things inside of me. These episodes were a turning point in my life. At that time it seemed a very hard turning point, but in the long run it was a good one. I felt the Lord's hand in the summer's events, and I knew that I had been protected from more threatening disasters in my life than I could probably imagine. However, I was struggling to heal a broken heart, and I became somewhat skeptical about my future life for a while. It almost seemed I was watching a strange movie or reading someone else's story. I felt as if Heavenly Father had suddenly and unexpectedly turned the wheels of the vehicle in which I was traveling through life and had changed my planned route. Through all the confusion, loneliness, and sadness I experienced after the summer, I was most grateful for the Lord's light inside my heart and the testimony that I would be all right.

I found myself in the stage of my life when I didn't know exactly what my new life path would be. But I knew with certainty that my life was in the Lord's hands and that it was up to me to appreciate his blessings and protection and learn from my experiences. After my exhausting and frightening experience with the police, I gained new strength and testimony in one area of my life—I stopped being fearful of Communists for good. A scripture that took new meaning for me was "For behold, you should not have feared man more than God. Although men set at naught the counsels of God, and despise his words—yet you should have been faithful; and he would have extended his arm and supported you against all the fiery darts of the adversary; and he would have been with you in every time of trouble" (D&C 3:7–8).

I finished my university studies, received two masters degrees—one in physical education and the other in pedagogy—and applied for the Ph.D. program. I struggled to find a job in Brno, but I insisted on staying in the city because of the expanding missionary work there. I couldn't find a job at any school until one day I saw a printed advertisement in the newspaper about a job at an organization called "House of Children and Youth." It was located in a beautiful park just five minutes by bus from where I lived. The building used to be an old summer mansion for Catholic nuns, but the Communists in Brno had taken it over and changed it into a center for children and youth activities after school hours. It was a place consisting of many different departments: tours, art, ballet, theater, computer science, biology, and many others. However, I soon learned that it was ideologically focused on the young future generation of Communists.

This fact didn't faze me. It wasn't any surprise to me, nor did I feel particularly disappointed or unfortunate, to have to deal with an organization that would have a heavy Communist influence. That was just a part of real life in Czechoslovakia. No one could avoid direct or indirect involvement with the existing Communist powers while working in the country during those days, no matter what the job.

When I saw the mansion, it occurred to me to organize yoga classes there and find a way to teach good life principles. But if someone had told me that day that the place would eventually become one of the largest yoga centers in the Czech Republic, I wouldn't have believed it.

I entered the office of the director of the House of Children and Youth, and I immediately guessed what type of person I would be talking with. The walls were decorated with Communist materials and pictures depicting the victory of Communism. When I talked to the director, a middle-aged Communist woman, about applying for a job, she said there would soon be a job opening in one of the departments. We talked about my skills, education, and background, and I could see that she was quite interested in my qualifications. She told me that she would contact me within a few days.

However, when I came the next time, she told me that the job she had mentioned wouldn't be offered until next year. I thought that was her way of telling me, "Sorry, we're not interested." But then she offered me another job, this one in the methodology department. I didn't have a clue as to what such a department was all about. I asked her a few questions and found out that it was the only department directly connected with the Communist Youth Organization. People at that department were creating goals, directions, and a future vision for Czech youth at all the schools in Brno, focusing on after-school activities. The department was thus connected to every school in Brno. I learned that there were about eighty-five elementary schools in the city, each with about one thousand pupils. My main responsibility, in conjunction with other members of the department, would be to organize seminars, lecture at these seminars, and create programs for the youth.

The stranger the idea looked, the more I knew that it was the place to be! I was hungry to learn organizing skills within a big organization like the Youth Organization. It would be a good skill for me to learn for our missionary efforts, which were rapidly expanding. Although I would work directly for the branch of Communist education of the youngest children in the country, I saw an excellent opportunity to learn helpful skills in working with young people while simultaneously practicing all the necessary organization and management skills. I believed that I could greatly benefit from observing things from within this unique environment.

I learned that I would even have the chance to write not only reports but also articles in local newspapers. I felt it was the right job in my present circumstances, and I decided to accept it. Even if I see a lot of negatives, I thought, I still can learn a lot. It turned out to be a good strategy. During the years I worked there, I learned a great deal from the many Communist failures I observed, as well as from the good examples I saw around me.

While observing and learning new skills for a few months, I felt more and more convinced that in our role as activity planners we could offer more meaningful activities for young people than I saw being offered. I had a wonderful boss, a young lady in her mid-thirties with many wonderful skills in working with people, and she was very open-minded. Although a member of the Communist party, she was a humble and trusting person with high moral values. I learned from her that she had joined the party a long time ago, while being strongly influenced and pressed to make the decision by other people around her. She regretted this "mistake of a lifetime" greatly and suffered from depression. Whenever she came back from a Communist meeting, I could see her self-image was devastated, and her face looked tense and afraid. It usually took her a few days to come back to herself. I tried to help her by encouraging her to cut down on coffee and quit smoking. She did so immediately. We became very close friends, and I visited her and her husband and daughter almost every week. I shared my yoga experience with her, and she became interested in taking my classes. Her health improved drastically, and she was grateful for this positive life change.

When I had completed my first year of working at the organization, I came to her with a plan. I wanted to start writing a monthly newsletter that would reach all the teachers and professors at all levels of the school system in Brno.

"You have my support one-hundred percent," she said and gave me some directions for achieving the goal.

The time was highly favorable to do this, because the general mood and attitude of people in my country was tense at the time. In the mid- to late 1980s, Eastern European Communist leaders were facing ever-increasing challenges. Through government reforms, Soviet leader Mikhail Gorbachev gave somewhat more freedom within the Soviet Union and also more responsibility to individual Communist leaders for governing their own countries, including Czechoslovakia. However, the Czech leaders didn't know what to do with this newfound opportunity. We watched them give outlandish, muddled speeches. In our country, the idea of Communism was disappearing, fading every day. Times became more open, and even the Communists themselves became critical and judgmental of each other as never before. Any disunity that had been among them before was even more visible to every citizen.

More than ever before, Czech people were willing and open to listen to and accept meaningful life values. The reason was simple: many Communist iniquities were pointed out almost every day in the newspapers and other media. The morality and integrity of local and national government leaders had taken a giant nose-dive through the years of Communism, and in the 1980s the Communists found themselves in a stage at which they had to publicly admit their mistakes because it was unbearable even for them to hide their sins any longer. However, their partial "public repentance" didn't make their image any better but only served to worsen it. It was too little, too late. The Czech people had a good memory of all their lies through the years, and so they understood that the Communists acted now only from a pure sense of necessity. But the political turmoil of the times was a good thing in that it began to change many Czech people's attitudes. Some of them came to believe slowly but surely that there must exist and prevail real truth in Czech history one day. It was just a question of time.

It was a good time to talk about ethics and morality in the pure sense of these topics. In my newsletters I saw a great chance to address at least one certain group—the public school teachers in Brno schools. I believed it was time to act, although I faced severe obstacles in the fact that sooner or later, as my ideas moved up the ladder of command for approval, my plan would have to be given the OK by some very old-fashioned Communist leaders.

I decided to fast and pray that I would be able to write the newsletter and thus continue my work of spreading some hope and good cheer, perhaps even planting a few seeds of gospel truth. When I came into the office of the Communist ideology leader to talk about the possibility of publishing a newsletter, he at first seemed uninterested. It was hard to judge from his face what his reaction to my proposal would be in the end. I took a few of his own quotations from some meetings where he had publicly spoken about bad morals among the people, and I then proposed a monthly newsletter to be called *Umění žít*—"Art of Living." I explained to him that the newsletter would introduce a few basic moral issues such as integrity, honesty, truthfulness, trust, morality, and so forth, as well as topics regarding positive life attitude, dealing with stress, and creating effective work schedules. It seemed to me that he was not necessarily against such a project but had trouble seeing any good that could come of it.

"What do you want to achieve with this newsletter?" he said as he raised his eyebrows.

"That our teachers can be more proactive in their personal life approach, as well as more helpful to young people."

"Isn't it a little bit too high an expectation you have?"

"I don't think so. It's something as important as having good teaching skills."

"But how would you introduce a topic like honesty or trust?"

I explained to him that I would take some quotations from well-known philosophers on a topic and would use Czech or foreign fables to illustrate the wisdom and truth of a value. It was very helpful to show him my first manuscript of a sample newsletter, which gave him a clearer picture of my proposal. He looked at the papers and after reading a few of my ideas, he abruptly said, "We shall see. I will let you know soon." My boss had a long conversation with him afterwards, and we succeeded in getting his approval the next day. All the necessary papers for the publishing were ready within four weeks, and I started writing.

The work became a real joy for me. Finally I was creating something meaningful to replace the usual Communist nonsense. We started with just one thousand copies in the beginning, but newsletter circulation spread not only in Brno but all over Moravia and many big cities in Bohemia. Each month the circulation was raised by a few hundred copies. After a few volumes were published, our methodology department got phone calls from the schools inviting me to come and give lectures on topics introduced in the newsletters. In addition, I had regular opportunities to speak at our organized seminars for teachers and professors during the school year at our department, and I was often invited to demonstrate some useful yoga exercises for general health as well. People apparently liked the unique combination and became very interested. After a few more months, I opened two yoga classes in the House of Children and Youth. Not too bad for a little Communist organization, I thought.

The following school year I lectured at universities in Brno and brought the unusual topic of morality to young university students. I greatly enjoyed working with them. Of course, there were those who were "too smart" to listen to me, but a great number of young adults were ready to hear that life could be more meaningful and might actually have the purpose of experiencing joy.

Things were happening in the Church in Czechoslovakia, too.

A new spiritual goal was set for priesthood holders and any Church members who wanted to join them. Brother Jiří Šnederfler, the Prague branch president, encouraged the brethren to fast every third Sunday for the purpose of obtaining official government recognition for The Church of Jesus Christ of Latter-day Saints in Czechoslovakia. We always had prayed for spiritual freedom in our country, but now we joined in a dedicated, focused, and prayerful effort. As Church members, we felt connected together as never before. A visit of President Monson gave Eastern European Latter-day Saints tremendous encouragement and hope for a better future.

By 1987, the Church had harvested many new converts around the country. A few people were joining the Church in Slovakia as well. These members traveled four hours almost every week to attend Sunday meetings in the Brno branch.

Legal government recognition of the Church was discussed among all the members. We felt that the political situation was more in our favor than ever during the past forty years. However, no one knew whether or not it was possible to achieve great, sweeping changes of religious freedom within a Communist government, and we had no way of knowing if there would be any political change in the country. Nobody could predict what exactly would happen.

Many Czech Latter-day Saints would lose their jobs if they admitted that they were Christian. I was one of them. I knew that if I openly announced to the Communists that I was a member of the Church, my career would be in jeopardy—particularly because I worked with the Czech younger generation and because I wrote the widely circulated newsletters. It was a real test for many of the members to see this new openness gradually evolving in our country. Some Church members liked the Church the way it had been for years in Czechoslovakia—underground. If nobody knew about their Church membership, they felt safer. I felt this strange new era was a real test of our faith.

"What am I going to do if they fire me?" asked one young sister. "I completed my university studies to be a teacher, but a teacher cannot believe in God in this country. What would I do if I had to openly declare my Church membership?" Questions like these became a new topic among converts.

My member-missionary efforts kept me busy in my after-work hours. Several of us traveled to many cities with Brother Vojkůvka and other members, opening new yoga classes, gently preparing participants to receive the gospel, and then helping people prepare for baptism. At that point I had had the privilege of preparing about forty people for baptism since my own conversion.

Because I was still working on getting a Ph.D. at the university in Brno, I had quite a busy schedule in order to accomplish all I needed to do. I got up every morning around four o'clock and studied, then put in a full day of work, then did as much member-missionary work as I could in the evenings and on weekends. It was the most disciplined time I had ever experienced.

I finally reached the end of my college studies and prepared to take the final examinations preparatory to receiving my Ph.D. One part of the Ph.D. exam was a detailed knowledge of the whole Marxist-Leninist philosophy, and in fact most of the candidates failed just because of this section of the exam. My guardian angels must have called in the reserves the day I took that exam, because the professors were hurling detailed, tricky questions at me as if I were a dart board with Ronald Reagan's face on it. I was exhausted afterwards, and frankly, I thought that I hadn't passed the exam because there were a few questions that stumped me. But I did pass! I could proceed with examinations in other subjects, and I was very happy when I completed the whole program and finally received a Ph.D. in pedagogy.

The most gratifying moment for me was to watch my parents as I was graduating. They were so happy for me. I was the first person in our family to receive a Ph.D, and I realized that for my

COMMUNIST ORGANIZATION • 1 5 7

parents, my graduation represented a gift in exchange for all the sacrifices and limitations they had faced during their lives of compromising with Communism.

The most interesting thing that happened at my work after I received the degree was that the Communists changed their behavior towards me. They became polite and respectful. There was a difference when I spoke up, and they were willing to listen to me with interest. I gained more freedom to present my ideas publicly in addresses and in the newsletter, and from then on I was able to be more specific about moral values in my writing and speaking.

14

THE VELVET REVOLUTION

A couple of years went by, more yoga classes were successfully opened, and even my boss—the woman who had helped me start the newsletter—began teaching yoga. Then November 1989 arrived, and the Velvet Revolution. I couldn't believe that anything like a revolution could happen in my country. I was in shock and the first two days could hardly believe the news.

It was Sunday evening and I was traveling to Brno as usual on the weekend. I was standing at a station in Brno to take a bus to my apartment. The station was close to the Mahen Theater and I could see dozens of police cars driving around. I thought it must be on fire.

"Hi, Olga. What do you think?" a young neighbor approached me when I got on the bus. She lived a few blocks from me, and we saw each other almost every day on the bus.

"What do you mean?" I asked. She appeared to be excited about something.

"Well, about the revolution!" she whispered into my ear.

"What kind of a revolution are you talking about? Where?"

"In Czechoslovakia, in Prague—here!"

"OK," I said. "What other joke do you want to play on me this weekend?" I was laughing and turned my face toward the window and looked outside.

"No joke. Reality. Did you see all those police cars around the theater? Prague actors started a strike and it has been spreading through all the other theaters in the country." She was speaking and I could sense that her breath was shortened. I still couldn't believe the words she was saying.

"Do you have a fever or what?" I asked her, agitated.

"I am not going to say another word to you." She leaned sideways and looked out of the window opposite mine.

Suddenly it was my body I thought was on fire, not the theater. I looked over the bus and could see that although some people were sitting silently, as usual, with no interest in what was happening around them, a number of people on the bus were talking about something which I couldn't understand exactly. But from their gestures and faces it appeared to me that my friend was truly speaking of something serious and very new to my ears and to my heart.

I arrived at my apartment, turned the TV on—everything looked normal, no sign of a revolution. I turned the radio on and didn't learn anything exciting. The newspapers looked boring as usual, except for the sports news.

The next morning, just when I entered the door at work, I could see the confused-looking members of the Communist party running here and there in the hallway.

"Hi," I said as I opened the door to my office. Only my boss was there.

"Oli, something really serious is going on in Prague. I have an emergency meeting right away—must go," she said, all in one breath, and she left the office within a few seconds. Other members of the department came and filled me in on the new information from Prague.

The reality of the situation hit me with full force: *It's true.*

There is a revolution! I felt amazement, shock, but the idea slowly entered my body, and my breath stopped for a few seconds.

Within one hour, a big meeting was held for the rest of us non-Communist types. When I entered the meeting room a moment before the whole organization had assembled, I sensed a feeling of great confusion, as if a huge question mark was hanging over everyone's heads as they sat in their chairs.

I noticed the Communist leaders of the school. "They look like drenched chickens," I whispered to one of my co-workers.

"They really do," she replied, and we exchanged smiles. Their faces truly were changing color. They looked red or white, depending, I suppose, on which emotion they felt most strongly at the moment—anger or fear.

One of the Communists stood up, and an official announcement was made: "There are some minor troubles in Prague. The actors don't want to perform and the students are hanging out on the streets instead of being at school, but we expect that it will be resolved today. We want to encourage you to remain calm and reassure your students that everything is stable and that nothing bad will happen." This was the Party line.

Within twenty-four hours, shop windows in the city were filled with all types of different messages from Prague, and eventually the Brno people were asked to join the general strike. It was an exciting and dangerous time all at once. The bitter memories from Prague 1968 held a lot of people back.

"Is it going to be a similar disappointment? Will people suffer afterwards like before?" people asked each other. It was difficult for many of us at work, Communist or non-Communist. No one knew how to act or what to say. Many people had been killed and put in prison during the Prague Spring in 1968. Their families had been heavily persecuted as politically incorrect citizens. Nobody could predict what would happen this time in 1989. A few people at work started wearing the tricolors of red, white, and blue—the sign of joining the revolution. A young woman, a co-worker who was working in the art department, was making inch-square tricolors out of clay.

"May I make my own?" I asked her. I had never worked with clay before.

"Sure, I'll teach you," she said with a smile. I had clay up to my elbows within a minute.

"This is where my revolution starts," I whispered, and we smiled. I had to try a few times to work the clay properly, but finally I made a few small tricolors for myself and my family.

The day of a general strike came. Obviously, the hard-headed old Communists didn't go, some people stayed at home, and a good number of the rest of us marched to the main square in Brno.

We walked through the Brno streets, joining other Brno citizens—organizations, colleges, universities, companies, and factory workers. People appeared to be so alive and focused. Yes, there was an excitement in the air, but simultaneously I could sense an unpredictable spirit of uncertainty. There was no assurance of future success, only hope in people's hearts. As we walked and gathered at the main square, policemen surrounded us, and in each corner of the square, water cannons were wheeled towards us. Even the policemen looked uncertain, however, as if this was something new even for them.

Within a few minutes, some Prague and Brno actors joined with a few university students and addressed the crowd. During their speeches, which were focused on impeaching the Czech Communist government immediately, people started shouting, "Demisi, demisi!" Some of the crowd took their keys from their pockets, started shaking the keys in their hands, and shouted, "Poslední zvonění! Poslední zvonění!"—"The final bell tolls! The final bell tolls!"—which was meant to let the Communists know that their time was up and that they must resign from political office.

As the speeches progressed, I sensed that all the people gathered around me were gaining more courage. Their faces depicted something so unusual, something that had not been seen in my country for years: people were actually smiling as a whole, and their faces were alive and more relaxed, although focused with every cell of their being on the words of the speakers. A new history was born in our blood, and the long-held shadows on our faces were wiped away that day. That was the most beautiful moment, as if the sun of meaningful Czech history had risen again, and an unexpected rainbow of promising victory had brightened the moment.

When the national anthem, "Kde domov můj!"—"Where is my home?"—filled the square, people held their hands together, some of them even kneeling down on the ground. A beautiful, liberating river of tears was falling down everyone's face. My heart pounded quickly. I knew I was witnessing the greatest moment of Czech history in my lifetime. I found myself singing the anthem, and for the first time in my life, the hymn's words were singing through my heart with meaning and resonating through my whole soul. For the first time in my life I felt that I was Czech, that my heart was Czech, and that the place I was born was my country, where my heritage belonged.

I had never felt that way before. A feeling of belonging to my country was born that very day. This healing birth took just the length of the anthem. I was grateful to feel in my soul the precious power of belonging to my country, the pure pulse of my Czech citizenship beating in my heart. The Czech roots of my ancestors were awakened inside of me. This experience became a treasure which I knew could never be taken away. For the first time in my life I felt happy that I was born in Czechoslovakia. I realized how beautiful Czech people are in their hearts and what a unique heritage they possess. I looked around me while singing the national anthem, and I could see that through people's suffering wrinkles, inner dread, and despair, a new hope of life was coming forth in that very moment.

I thought about all the horrible times in my country—in my generation, my parents' and grandparents' generations—the tragedies which we had to witness for so many years while being oppressed by Communist propaganda and all the evil the government caused to Czech citizens. But even my perspective of those tragedies felt different, somehow—not as important in that moment of new happiness and inner joy that was rising in my country. I was just profoundly happy to be standing in the square and feeling such joy at that moment.

Above all this renewal that I experienced in the space of only a few minutes of my life, a more amazing renewal went through my spirit. There was the Spirit of God among the people, no question about it! There was unity, there was love, a mutual understanding, unselfishness, togetherness—nothing was holding back the beautiful Spirit. It didn't matter if people believed in God or not, knew about the reality of God or not in that point in time; still they were reflecting God's love. I recalled Paul's words: "Where the Spirit of the Lord is, there is liberty" (2 Corinthians 3:17). For a brief second I thought about Enoch and his people who were taken to heaven as a whole society of Zion.

The atmosphere of hope remained for months among the people. It was such a change to see Czech people alive, discussing life and national matters together on trains, buses, and streets while smiling and helping each other.

Everyone was so grateful and proud at the same time that the Czech revolution was christened by the world as "the Velvet Revolution." A new government was installed and a new life began peacefully without warfare or weapons. It was truly a miracle of God!

Of course, some individuals clung to the old selfishness and the sickness of Communist life which had penetrated through their minds and hearts. Real life and a new history began in my country, but many Czech people didn't want to understand that newborn freedom in Czechoslovakia would require individual, long-term sacrifice.

Within the few months after the revolution, the House of Children and Youth, including the methodology department where I worked, faced the challenge of either survival or failure. It became a failure. There was no further need for an organization focused on future Communist youth. I found this unique situation to be a great advantage in building a yoga department, which had been almost about to happen before the revolution. We continued to build up a team of yoga teachers—many of them members of the Church in the Brno branch—and we began to teach basic Christian moral principles in many Brno high schools and also universities, embedding these truths in a yoga context. My boss gained a certificate for yoga teaching and was very excited about the whole idea. The most important fact was that the interest in our unique yoga teaching spread and actually became a welcome source of income for the organization. Right after the revolution, she and I made an advertisement for more classes and offered them also to the public in Brno. Within a few months we had a number of new teaching groups, each of them with about fifty students.

A plan for a new department was developed within a few days. A new head of the organization was chosen, and this new boss made me the manager. My old boss, now a good friend, and I worked together as a harmonious team.

This was the opportunity I had always dreamed of! Because all the Communist ideology was immediately taken out of the schools, there was no remaining school program that was focused specifically on developing moral principles. This was a wonderful blessing and opportunity, because the schools asked for our yoga lectures to fill the void. We had the chance to bring a lot of good ideas into the schools before any kind of stringent system could be put into place. Also we could begin using a book we had written for these courses, *Self-Education in Ethics and Morality*. This book incorporated positive life principles based on gospel principles, although we didn't advertise them as the gospel. I found that all my previous experience with yoga camps was very helpful; once again, we were dealing with nonbelievers, this time with young, materialistic-minded, atheistic students. They were sharp and very critical at the same time, like any teenagers who lack any meaningful moral and ethical education, having no good family principles established and lots of bad examples around them.

But once the students began to accept moral principles one by one, they began to see the holes in their logic and some of the mistakes they had made in life up to that point. It was truly a miraculous thing to create and witness the effects of this system all at once. A few of these teenagers accepted the gospel and were baptized. Although our lectures in the schools were of limited duration, we felt a tremendous sense of accomplishment after having done this for one whole school year.

My boss and I became not only a great team but also dear friends. She knew about my Church membership and respected many religious ideas. Right during the crisis of the revolution, she had denounced her membership in the Communist party. I went with her to the office when she told the leader about her intentions to leave the party once and for all. He was shocked. It was still during the time when nobody knew what would actually happen over the next twenty-four hours. It was not obvious that the revolution would end up on the people's side. She was so brave.

"Olga, this is the most important day in my life," she told me before she walked into the office.

"I know that this is the best gift you have ever given to yourself in your life," I replied. Within a few minutes she was out of the office, and I could see she was nervous, her face red and tense.

"I did it! I cannot believe it! I did it!" she said. I gave her a big hug and looked for a peaceful place, where I offered a prayer. She was so grateful for the prayer and told me, "Olga, it is amazing, all the heaviness of my life is gone. I can feel it. I am so happy that I had the strength to finish this part of my life, regardless of the consequences which could follow in the future. I know it is right. I am healthy again and as free as in my youth." She expressed gratitude for the part I had played in helping her make this decision, and we cried with happiness together.

Today this good woman is the head of Brno's city-sponsored yoga department, which is the largest of its kind in the country. The good moral and ethical seeds I helped plant in the department during the days of Communism have grown and taken root and are still blossoming. The department became a training center for all the yoga teachers in the country. She has been organizing seminars on a national level and oversees a large number of different yoga clubs in Brno. I am grateful to our Heavenly Father that he helped our paths cross and that through our work partnership and the Lord's inspiration, we were able to build something that has had a lasting positive effect on the Czech people.

15

AMERICA FOR
THE FIRST TIME

The Velvet Revolution in 1989 signified a tremendous change for all Czech Latter-day Saints. No longer was it necessary to keep the blinds pulled down when we gathered for church meetings, all of us in fear of being thrown into prison. The times truly had changed. Although the Church was still waiting to be officially recognized, the Church leaders were visiting the Czech government frequently for this purpose, and everyone knew that our constant prayers and fasts were being answered and that the doors would be opened again for the Church.

One of the most significant blessings and changes came to the Czech members several years before the Velvet Revolution when the Freiberg Temple in East Germany was dedicated in June 1985. After the temple was opened, many worthy Czech members had the opportunity and the privilege to enter the temple. The temple ordinances were translated into Czech before the temple was opened, but it was after the temple's opening that audiovisual materials used in presenting the temple endowment were translated into Czech. To do this, it was necessary to bring a team of Czech members to Salt Lake City. Many members' voices were taped and sent to Church headquarters in Utah, and some of these members, including myself, were asked to come to Salt Lake City and assist in preparing the filmed portion of the temple presentation.

I flew to Salt Lake City in September 1990, hardly believing the stamp in my passport which allowed me to enter the United States. I, who hadn't even been allowed to visit the Soviet Union? I reflected on all the pain and fear I had felt during the incident with the Czech police only a few years earlier. I felt like a small child, opening the page of the passport numberless times just to reassure myself that my U.S. trip was a reality and not a dream. I had always desired to visit America, especially since my becoming a Latter-day Saint, but I never thought that it would actually happen.

As the plane in which I traveled neared Salt Lake City, I saw the city below, shining but also miraculously hidden in the middle of the mountains. Moments later I was standing at the Salt Lake City airport, being greeted by a few Czech members living in Salt Lake who had come to greet us and welcome us.

One of my most surprising first impressions after landing in Salt Lake City was the feeling of enormous space around me, a great sense of a well-organized work as well as the cleanliness that met my eye. I felt not only surrounded but also embraced by the majestic Utah mountains. I looked out from my hotel windows the evening we arrived, and the city looked like a small kingdom of lights. My soul was immersed in gratitude to witness such unusual beauty.

As a Latter-day Saint I rejoiced to be in the very place which represented the heart of the Church. This first arrival meant something similar to me in my own way, I believe, as the pioneers' arrival in the Salt Lake Valley must have meant to them. Before my coming to Utah, the largest group of Latter-day Saints I had ever seen in one place numbered close to one hundred. Here I was in a place where a large percentage of the citizens were my brothers and sisters in the gospel! Here was the home of the Tabernacle Choir, which I admired greatly and which I had so far heard only on a few cassette tapes. Every minute brought something new for me to absorb, to observe, to dive into again and again as I breathed this new environment into my heart.

I remember wondering, What is it like to live among other members of the Church? How would it be to have at least one neighborhood in my country where many Latter-day Saints would live together? What difference would it make in their lives and in the neighborhood itself?

Because my first visit was focused directly on doing special Church work for my fellow Saints, my mind was occupied and centered on the spiritual environment in which I found myself. I stayed in America only about ten days in all, and most of my time was spent in a recording studio in the Salt Lake Temple. Therefore, my vision of America was initiated among the most delightful, spiritual, highly educated, humble and respectful of Church members. It was a real joy to be surrounded by people fully devoted to the Lord's work and strong in their testimony of Christ. I treasure that special occasion as one of the most beautiful times of my life. Those wonderful temple workers instilled in me an overwhelming sense of the great worth of the work we were doing for our brothers and sisters back in Czechoslovakia. I had never had such a chance to work under the delightful influence of a pure spirit of love and mutual cooperation.

All the work we did to prepare the Czech temple materials during those ten days created in my heart a very high picture of the rest of the Utah members. I met wonderful people, each of them a great personal model for me in some way or another.

One of the marvelous opportunities during the visit was to attend general conference in the Tabernacle. The Tabernacle reminded me of Europe more than anything else in Salt Lake City, especially because it represented a connection of many generations past and present, which is so common to the European historical edifices. Buildings like this always carry not only a sense of history but also the evidence of how this history is being lived out in the present day.

This was represented to me by a little boy who was sitting next to me, embraced in the arms of his father. It was another miracle to me to learn that anyone living in Utah, all over the USA, or in many other nations could turn the TV on and watch the proceedings of the most important and valuable meetings of all the earth. I understood very little because of my limited English, but the amount of the Spirit of God that I could absorb was a cleansing and healing power which poured through me, thanks to the Spirit and those who spoke. If I didn't ever again see anything else in my life of Church headquarters except that conference and the influence and impact those sessions had on me, I knew that my life would still have gained a new perspective and vision. The great spirit of the conference wasn't anything obvious to the mortal eye, but it was very simple in occurrence and most powerful for the believing heart and spirit. The combination of the conference addresses and the beautiful music of the choir represented to me the literal dispersal of the word of God. I was witnessing the way our modern scriptures of today are delivered to my heart the same as in the times of Moses, Abraham, Enoch, Benjamin, or Alma as they spoke to their contemporaries.

I couldn't have witnessed a more important event during those two days of my life. I felt as if I were a part of the living history of the gospel. I wondered what these Church events must mean for all the members from Utah and elsewhere who were able to listen with open hearts year in and year out. "There must be a lot a spiritual giants in the Church around the world," I marveled. "And what about those singers from the Tabernacle Choir, who not only can listen but are closer to the source of wisdom and God's servants than almost anyone else?" The spirit they evidenced in their singing was equal to the spirit I felt from the speakers.

During our visit we were invited to the Missionary Training Center in Provo one day. I didn't know that this visit would change my life forever. My first impression when I walked through the main MTC entrance was that there is no harder working place in the Church than that one. It reminded me of a perfectly organized beehive. There wasn't any facet of the facility that lacked a fine focus on the main mission of the place or that would engender any distracting or critical thoughts. The pattern of following correct principles was evident everywhere I moved or looked. The joy of life felt like a natural oxygen of the place.

We met a lot of wonderful leaders, teachers, and missionaries that day, and I learned that the existing Czech missionary training program had started just one year previous to that time, and the MTC leaders were looking for a Czech teacher who could help develop the teaching of the missionary discussions in the Czech language. Words led to other words, and I found myself in the situation of being considered to come for a half year and teach and participate in the creation of a new Czech program.

The proposal came as an unexpected lightning bolt from the sky, and my main concern was that I didn't speak English.

"Well, we don't need you to speak English, only Czech" was the quick answer. I was taken to Czech, French, and Spanish classes that day and learned that in each classroom at the MTC, the missionaries speak the foreign language no matter whether they are in the MTC for their first or last week of training. I marveled at this feat, which I had never witnessed in language teaching before. The other miraculous thing was that a majority of the teachers were young university students, not professors. I was totally amazed at what a mind focused on a high spiritual goal, together with enormous diligence and hard work, can achieve. I couldn't compare these young people to any other university students I had met before; their determination to achieve their goal was not only high, but the Spirit of the Lord was in their hearts, along with daily spiritual nourishment and the excitement of the important work to be done in the field.

Without any hesitation I decided to accept this wonderful offer. There also would be an opportunity for me to study English as a second language while teaching at the MTC. However, I wondered, as probably any Eastern European in my circumstances would have, how I could financially afford such a trip. My savings account back in Czechoslovakia was enough to buy a Czech car, but in the eyes of the Western world I could hardly afford an air ticket from my country to the United States, not to mention lodging. It seemed impossible, but I thought that if the Lord wanted me to come, he would help me find a way.

We returned to Salt Lake City from the MTC. I sat in my hotel room and wondered what I should do. In addition to the other challenges, I would need a sponsor, which I didn't have. I knew a number of Utah members who by that point could be counted as friends, but I would be embarrassed to just pick up the phone and ask, "Hi there, would you be my sponsor?" I didn't even have the slightest idea as to how much five hundred or five thousand dollars meant for an American. However, I knew that I couldn't just pray and wait in my hotel room and see what would happen. Time was short; I had only about three days before leaving Salt Lake City and returning to Czechoslovakia. If I wanted to act, I needed to be quick.

The day before that, I had visited with a few other Czech members. With them was a couple from Salt Lake City whom I had recently met back in Czechoslovakia. They were Gordon and Carol Madsen. As we were leaving their home, Brother Madsen, a grandson of President Heber J. Grant, told me, "Olga, I believe we will see each other again." I thought it was a polite sentence, but I didn't realize that this family would later be willing to help me.

While I was kneeling at my hotel bed and praying, the Madsens' faces returned to my mind again and again. It took me hours to pick up my hotel phone and call their number, but it proved to be the most important phone call I had ever dialed in my life. I talked to Brother Madsen and told him in my hesitant English all about the offer I had received from the MTC, about studying English, and about my financial situation. I told him that I couldn't come to the United States without having a sponsor.

"I'll be in your hotel tomorrow in the morning. Can we meet in the lobby?" he quickly replied.

"Yes, I will be there."

The next morning when we met, he was holding a sponsorship paper in his hand with all the appropriate blanks filled in. As if that were not a stunning development, he also told me that he would help me purchase the air tickets. Within less than twenty-four hours, the wheels of my life turned in a different direction, toward a new destination I could scarcely imagine. I knew that missionary work was the Lord's work, but also I knew that without this miraculous, inspiring, timely, and Christlike assistance from a family who knew little about me and yet were willing to help me, all this would not have been possible.

There are people in our lives who make our personal history possible. The Madsens are in my book of life as just such people. Thanks to their help, a new chapter of my life began. Later I learned that the same family helped two other wonderful Czech members, whom they met in Czechoslovakia, to serve full-time missions. One of them served a mission in the United States and the other in England. I learned an important lesson from this family, who were not only smiling and nice but were sincerely ready and willing to help.

Before I left the States, I met Sister Carol Lee Hawkins, a member of the Relief Society General Board.

"We would love to have you come and speak at the women's conference at BYU next April!" she said.

I thought she was joking in light of the fact that I didn't speak much English. How could I possibly speak in front of people just six months from now? Not in front of a hundred people but before an audience of thousands? I didn't know what to say. She obviously could hear my very limited English abilities. But she was serious. She actually seemed to be more confident about me than I was myself. I learned later on that Carol has been always a woman of action and that many miracles can really happen around her, thanks to her clear vision and her brave personality.

"Well, when you come back to America we will speak about it in more detail" were her last words as she was hugging me, smiling, and saying good-bye.

As I traveled home to Czechoslovakia in the airplane, I contemplated my future. A new semester would be starting at BYU in January. I had just about two months to prepare myself to go for a half-year visit to the United States. My life picked up new speed, and I was hardly able to absorb all the other wonderful news connected with my future trip.

Our Czech Mission President, Richard Winder, came to me soon after I arrived back home and offered me specific help, which came from his daughter, Susan Tanner, and her husband, John. I learned that they lived in Provo and had offered to let me stay in their house while studying at BYU and teaching at the MTC. I was deeply moved as I realized how many wonderful people—some of whose names I didn't even know—were involved in making the great opportunities of the future possible for me.

When December 12, 1990, arrived, I was in Prague at the mission home with all the necessary documents to enter the United States again. We had a wonderful dinner prepared by Sister Winder, and we shared a sort of farewell with President Winder and the missionaries. As I rested later that evening, I thought, Tomorrow I will be in the airplane to Frankfurt, and the day after tomorrow I will be landing in Salt Lake City. I was still surprised that something like this was happening in my life. I also realized that this would be my last night in my homeland for a while.

The next morning as I was sitting at the Prague airport, sadly watching small snowflakes change to huge ones, I began worrying about the weather. Within a couple of hours, the Prague airport runways were covered with about four inches of new snow. Poor flying conditions in Frankfurt were announced, and I learned that my plane would have at least a two-hour delay. I knew I would be late for the following flight connection, from Frankfurt to Cincinnati, and I didn't have any idea as to how these situations were handled at airports.

"Your airline company will take care of you," a lady at the information desk told me. My plane landed late in the afternoon in Frankfurt. The airport was packed with people running in all different directions. Apparently, many flights were canceled that day, and everyone was busy and confused trying to find a way to their destinations. I was one of those confused ones—perhaps the most confused one, I should say—and felt hopeless. I must have looked funny, like a frightened rabbit in the middle of the road. "Hey, everybody's gone through something similar in life. So what?" I murmured, trying to encourage myself. I didn't know where to go, what to do, or who to ask for help. After asking a few basic questions of a German policeman, I walked to check my next-day flight possibilities. The lines were hopelessly long, and it was almost midnight when I caught a taxi to a hotel as had been arranged by the airline company.

Kind of a strange beginning, I thought when I finally got to my hotel room, exhausted and not knowing what to expect tomorrow, but I made it. The next day when I was happily sitting in the airplane on my way to the United States, I reflected that the hectic day before seemed a long time ago. I resolved that because the speed of every minute was new to me, I would be more focused on the present and not look back too much.

The Madsens were waiting for me at the airport, and they drove me to their home, which became my shelter for a few weeks. This period was my real introduction to American life. I wasn't in a hotel but in a real home. Carol took me downtown to see Salt Lake City again. I was shocked. It was Christmastime and my eyes bugged out at the bright red colors of this season so typical for America. It was beautiful, but it was scary too. I had always connected the color red with the Soviet Union and Communists—and here I faced it at Christmastime! I saw gold stars at the top of Christmas trees, which reminded me of Russian Communist stars.

I am sick, I thought, or this is just a bad dream—or maybe I am paralyzed from Communism. I couldn't share these ideas with anyone, but they were rankling thorough my entire soul. This new world was too strong a reality for an Eastern European to digest.

I was amazed to see small children playing Christmas songs in the big Salt Lake City downtown mall. The city's Christmas decoration was visually overwhelming with all beautiful colors, shapes, and atmosphere. I had never witnessed anything like that. I wasn't able to stay in the mall more than an hour or so, because it was just hard to absorb the uncountable quantity of all the different products.

My brain is going crazy, I realized after walking through the mall a while and seeing all the shops. I could spend hours just looking in a candy store at all the different types of goodies, and I marveled that Americans had mastered the art of finding a way to satisfy every possible human pleasure in the form of a salable product.

"It would take me one whole year just to explore all the different flavors and combinations of American ice creams and frozen yogurts," I said, laughing as I ordered a small chocolate frozen yogurt. Although I ordered the small size, I thought the saleswoman must have made a mistake: to my Czech eyes, it seemed the serving must certainly be the large size.

"It's all right," she said. Well, I learned quickly that American portions of ice cream are the most generous I have ever seen in my

life. Little did I know then that there were Super Big Gulps waiting for me at the 7-Eleven!

I was a typical Czech or Eastern European coming to the
Western capitalist world without having had any previous experiences to prepare me. I had a feeling that I had COMMUNISM tat-
tooed all over my body, inside and out. The very first thing I
noticed about myself was that I found myself somehow lost, locked
in the armor of a long life of Communist influence around me. I
felt as if I were encased in a stiff body cast, with an overwhelming
feeling of a Capitalist Monster chasing me around, in and out of
every shop and store. In addition I felt an alarming sense of ignorance: I didn't know how to open my hotel room or turn the light
off and on, how to use an elevator or open a car door, or how to eat
some kind of fruit which I had never seen or tasted before. You
mean you really do eat tacos with your hands? I wondered as I
watched customers around me. It wasn't just a cultural shock. In
addition, each small thing witnessed to me how badly the whole
Communist system had closed people's lives and cut them off from
opportunities to grow as free people and to make their own decisions. I didn't particularly feel frustration—just amazement at the
material comfort which surrounded me. Even when I looked in the
jar of a homeless beggar on the street, I saw that he had made more
money during the hour since I had last passed him on my way to
the hotel than any Czech citizen would earn during a whole week.
Those kinds of things really made me think!

From the very first day, America to me could be summed up in
one sentence: "You have to make a choice!" This idea followed me
everywhere. It started in the grocery store, where the lady at the
counter would ask me, "Paper or plastic?" During my whole life
in Czechoslovakia, not once had I had to face such an earth-
shattering decision, and if I had, I probably would have answered,
"It doesn't matter" or "It's up to you." Just having two things to
choose from was a change. Most of the time I would have had

absolutely no choice in my homeland: there was one existing possibility or none at all. Any American citizen on his first business
trip to a big city would probably look more confident than I did
during those first few weeks in America. There was no question
that I found myself almost like a prisoner who had just obtained
freedom after thirty years and didn't realize how much life had
changed around him.

I spoke English just well enough to get around and not be
totally lost, and that obviously limited my explorations. In my
infrequent spare time, I would go to a bookstore. I love American
bookstores. I could just spend hours there! Americans, I reflected,
are so fortunate and blessed to have so much literature—books on
any topic a person can possibly imagine! I saw that there were
many different levels and qualities of writing, from the cheap, dis-
gusting "bottom of the barrel" to works that reflected the marvelous
apex of the human mind. It was incredible to me that so many
people had the opportunity to express themselves by writing books
focused on their own level of unique understanding. It didn't matter that what an individual would create with their own mind or
hands would actually appeal only to a small group of people.
American books were a vast display of the different pathways of
human lives, of writers with very divergent talents, whereas in my
country under Communist rule, the same individual writers would
suffer and their unique opinions would be lost because there
wouldn't exist any kind of field or discipline in which such a creative thinker could earn a living or even follow his line of thinking
as a hobby.

During the early part of my visit to the United States, my most
frequent purchases were books and postcards. My mom had always
teased me with the nickname "walking library" because wherever I
would go, I would always take at least two or three books with me.
Now that I was in a country where I could find all the books I could

imagine, my love of books led me to make a strong and adamant decision: "I must learn English."

The other things I discovered that were new to me and very American were cars. I just couldn't believe how many times I saw one person sitting in a car and driving on a highway. Such a waste of space, I thought.

"Why don't you have more buses? You wouldn't have so many traffic jams," I naively remarked to one of my American friends.

"We love our freedom to go places in our own time instead of being dependent on some bus."

"Even at the price of sitting on a highway in this incredible traffic?"

"Yep. You get used to it quickly."

I was surprised at how much every activity in American life—meetings, parties, dates, even going to see movies—was connected with food. It seemed to me that the most important decisions American people make, no matter if in business or private life, are made around lunch or dinner tables. I didn't know if it was rather my personal observance or a general point of view, but it seemed to me that Czechs work to eat. But Americans eat to work.

These were just a few of my first observations, purely from my Czech perspective. It wasn't easy to adapt to America's different ways, but it put me in a learning spirit every minute of the day, and I loved this challenge. The hardest hurdle, of course, was my language barrier. If I found myself in a large group of people who were talking and changing the topic at almost the speed of light, I found myself insecure, confused, tired, discouraged, and lost.

The American style of talking appeared to me very fragile, with each speaker in a conversation changing to a new topic as soon as possible, not going into depth on a single idea or topic. In a few minutes a group could move from talking about Africa to discussing what it was like growing up on a dairy farm. I would be asked, "Where are you from?" My answer might bring a request for more details, and right in the middle of my explanation, someone would bring up another and another question, turning the discussion to a completely different topic. I would wonder where this new topic came from—something like computers, the best restaurants in town, or movies. I was rarely able to finish what I wanted to say, and it often seemed that halfway through my comment, nobody was interested anymore, or they wanted to know only just one piece of information before moving on to another topic. It was very frustrating, and I had to accept it as a different culture and learn to respect it. But at the time, it seemed to me that Americans were so disrupted with all the stuff in the world around them that they could hardly stay focused. It was like surfing on the sea. It was a way of life.

On the other hand, I was amazed to see how productive individuals could be in this fast-paced country. That was the greatest lesson I learned within the first few weeks as I started to attend English classes and teach at the MTC.

Just a couple of days before Christmas, I moved to the Tanner family's home in Provo. The family took me under their wings with love from that day onward. John sacrificed his working room and office for my bedroom. I couldn't believe that I would actually have my very own room! I didn't expect such a comfort at all.

I greatly admired the way this family was organized and had an exact plan every day. They had five children: Jonathan, Bobbie, Becky, Elizabeth, and Maryanne. My usual experience with Czech kids was that they wouldn't pay so much attention to a visitor after a few days, but the Tanner kids were a different story, especially Elizabeth and Maryanne, the youngest ones. We often sang Czech songs at the piano. Elizabeth and Maryanne enjoyed my "horsey riding" so much that my knees were red almost every evening. They both had a grand laugh in the evenings when I read them some fables and fairy tales in English with my Czech accent. They taught me how to pronounce words, and we all laughed together.

Becky and Bobbie taught me important words and phrases like "cool," "awesome," "you bet," and so on. I couldn't manage to pronounce "cool" in their style, but they could mimic my Czech-accented English without any problem!

The best thing that happened to me while staying in the United States was to be placed in such a healthy spiritual environment as the home of this faithful Latter-day Saint family. It was a blessing, and it made such a big difference in the way I felt in a strange country. Living with the Tanners greatly increased my understanding of the importance of family life in the Church! I felt secure and at home. We got up at six o'clock every morning, started the day with a prayer, and followed with reading scriptures while having breakfast. Every day a warm dinner was served and everyone was around the table again. I was introduced to the Tanners' ward and was amazed that almost a hundred percent of their neighbors were not only members of the Church but members of the same ward. For those members it was a natural thing, but for me a pure miracle of God. When I had joined the Church in my country, I had traveled at least two hours to see another member of the Church, and here I could just walk next door.

I had never seen so many children in a ward as I saw in the Church in Utah. Primary class was packed with a number of children which would represent one whole branch in Czechoslovakia. I was amazed to see so many chapels. The strangest thing for me was singing in all the Sunday meetings. Within a month, I had no doubt sung as many hymns as I had during all the years of my Church membership in my homeland. At that time John had a calling in the Primary, and I was also amazed at that. If we had a member like him, he would be branch president right away, I thought. I was learning that the Lord's needs are different in each corner of the world.

CHAPTER

16

ON MY OWN
IN A NEW WORLD

There was so much to digest in the first months in the United States. I didn't know how to stop the bus and get off where I wanted, how to turn on the dishwasher, or how to tell a dime from a nickel. (Have you ever noticed that there are no numbers on U.S. coins?) And for a world superpower and bastion of democracy, America seemed to sell an awful lot of things made in China.

How should I answer the question "How are you?" I pondered after being in America a few days. I struggled with this greeting question. When someone asked me the question, which was about a hundred times a day, I would start to speak about my life. But soon I realized that this phrase was nothing more than a greeting, not a solicitation for information. How different from my language! I found myself many times with my mouth open, ready to respond; but before I was able to say anything, the person who had greeted me was already gone. It took me a long time to consider this question as a greeting and not an introduction to dialogue.

In addition, I frequently was asked the question, "What country are you from?" I found it really difficult to adjust to people's varying responses when I told them I was born and raised in Communist Czechoslovakia. When people responded, "Oh—from

Russia," I felt hurt and angry. How hard it was to hear that! The Russians were enemies to the United States. My new American friends must have thought that therefore my country, as a part of the socialist empire, had to be in that category also. How bitter! It upset me because I didn't ever feel connected to the Soviet Union, and I believe the majority of my countrymen did not either, although the political leaders in my country pronounced the Soviet Union to be our Eternal Friend.

My own feeling was not anything personal against the Russian people but instead was a dislike of the Russian government, which destroyed so many people's lives, talents, characters, beliefs, enthusiasm for life—their hopes.

It was interesting as I came to the United States after the Czech Velvet Revolution and met people from Russia. I felt immediate love for them, for one reason—I finally had the chance to meet ordinary Russian people with their genuine heritage and respect for life. These people were not a part of a monster but were real, deep-thinking, talented people.

My joy was even greater when I met a woman from Moscow who had been converted to the gospel. It was an amazing feeling of happiness to meet a Russian citizen with a deep testimony of the Church. Nothing can be more healing and purifying than the fulness of the gospel truths brought by the missionaries to our neighboring Slavic countries, where authentic friendship was natural once upon a time but had all but disappeared over many years of Soviet Communist rule.

During my first few months in America, I found myself totally exhausted by the end of the day from listening, concentrating, trying to reply in English, and absorbing the all-new information around me. In the long run, this was a great learning experience in a new culture, although at the time it was very difficult. In the beginning I felt very silly not knowing how to respond to the most basic question. It made me angry and frustrated, and I found myself in a strange imbalance, lacking in confidence, like a kid in first grade who doesn't say anything when the teacher asks, "What is your name?" It was a chance to find new sectors of my personality.

"I am not used to absorbing so many colors around me. Sometimes I feel like I'm in a circus and not in real life," I wrote to my parents. "My eyes hurt and my brain is going crazy!"

I was learning odd things about the American style of everyday life, things that were not only new but often surprising to me.

"It seems to me that everybody in this country has a dog or a cat. Is it the fashion?" I asked.

"Of course not," people would answer. And yet I was amazed to see in the grocery store an entire section of products just for cats and dogs, and later to see an advertisement for cat food on TV in which a cat was eating from a champagne glass! And when I saw an animal hotel in one town, I discovered a new face of America: "It is wild! American dogs and cats are treated like kings!"

I felt a busy working spirit wherever I went, whether I was among school children, teenagers, university students, or retired people.

"Every American watches his or her time," I remember writing to my friends in my homeland. "There is always and everywhere a sharp American look at the clock. Even in church, when someone speaks longer than he or she should, people are polite but don't seem to like it at all. Babies start crying and the entire assembly starts shifting in their seats, falling asleep, checking the clock, or just simply turning off their attention."

I really like that about America; I like organization and good use of time. However, I soon found myself becoming overly time-sensitive, and I didn't like the feeling of time stress. It felt awful to see that my life was revolving so much around time. The American approach to time was completely different from what I had experienced in Czechoslovakia. I felt back in my country that I could somehow stop in my tracks and relax for a while, but here I could pause for only a second before an idea of what should be done next would come suddenly shooting into my mind. I learned to love and appreciate weekends.

I learned that there was something completely different about Fridays. People were smiling, and even though they were still in a hurry, they knew there would soon be a couple of days for them not to just rest but, more particularly, to have fun.

I loved one thing I discovered about Americans—they know how to play and enjoy themselves when it comes to parties and leisure time. The Czech and American styles of fun and entertainment were completely opposite. I just loved watching Americans playing all different kinds of games, trying new sports, going to see different sporting events. I was especially delighted to see their love for gathering together as friends and family. That was new to me; Czech people living under the restraints of Communism actually didn't desire to be together. To be together with one another meant more stress. They could get into trouble if they drank a little too much or said something which could be used later against them. Therefore, togetherness wasn't the typical way to spend leisure time. Czech people would take a more individual approach with their leisure. They liked to be separated as much as possible from the outside world during the weekend—in a cabin somewhere, hiking in nature far from civilization, or staying in the basement and enjoying a hobby. I learned that in America everybody could act for himself or herself. Daily stress, business, homework, meetings, and all the other usual daily activities were "switched off" and left behind on the weekends as much as possible. I decided it's great to feel that kind of a separation for a few days.

I didn't find anything more personalized in the States than American cars. And the loud music! I always thought that only teenagers wanted to share their entertainment with the rest of the people on the road. And the bumper stickers. Oh, my, how the

Communists would have had a stroke over bumper stickers! It was hard to understand why people would like to put their religion, political opinion, or personal life credo on a car bumper! I wondered, Do the rest of us really care if you are a member of the Hot Sauce Club of America?

"More than ninety percent of bumper sticker messages I have seen would translate into an immediate prison stay for a Czech person under Communism," I shared with a friend of mine, and he laughed and couldn't understand that something so silly would bother Communists.

Well, at least people here have their freedom to show their ignorance or wisdom! I thought, but I also observed that in a free country, ideas and opinions without boundaries can easily cross a healthy line such that nobody pays attention anymore. I could see that even freedom could become boring—a casual, plain, ordinary matter of life, perhaps even taken for granted by some.

If I looked at a young Czech and a young American child, there wasn't any question that the material access any average American child has while growing up was far beyond that of a Czech child. The difference wasn't so much in basic needs such as food, shelter, or basic education, but rather in the speed of information and of constant progress in technology, which brings a broad advantage and opportunity to an American child. I had to remind myself that my country had been shut off from the entire world for a few decades.

Naturally it made me wonder who I would be if I had grown up in this country instead of in Czechoslovakia. How different would I be? How good or not-so-good would I be?

Young Americans were curious to find out how I felt about having new freedom in my homeland. However, after I would make even a few sentences of reply, even the Czech revolution would become a sleep-inducing topic for many of them. It made me think and ponder about life differently. So far I had seen only my country, the suffering of my people. As horrible as all that was, I also realized that there are people living in the beautiful and free United States who suffer because of their bad choices or because of circumstances brought on by life's offerings. I was grateful to Heavenly Father for opening my eyes and letting me see America's beauty of life as well the struggles. I had been naive—I had thought that everything must be perfect where people have their freedom. However, I realized that everyone is challenged differently, and life can consist of more than a fight for freedom!

Even the geographic layout of American cities was strange and new. A square in a Czech city always represents the heart of the city where people meet and hang out together. There is a cultural as well as a historical heritage to admire in that.

"Where is the main square?" I asked one day.

"What do you mean?"

"Well, the place where everybody goes to gather in your town, where history takes place."

"Oh, that's the baseball stadium!" was the answer. I had to laugh. I learned that cities in the United States are giant, with long miles of uncoordinated traffic lights, huge buildings, and lots of people hurrying and driving in all different directions. I had a hard time finding a feeling of belonging; everything and everybody seemed to be in constant movement.

However, when I went to the mall, I felt more at home. Although I had been confused by my first visits to shopping malls, I began to feel more at home when I visited them. I felt almost as if I had entered a city inside a city. Palm trees, benches, fountains, and stores were set up one next to the other, exactly like in any Czech city, but everything was under one roof.

One thing I missed badly was Czech bread—bread which is made from a sour dough with a hard crust, and not cut beforehand, so that after purchasing it you can cut as big a chunk as your taste demands. When I looked at the bread in American stores, two things came to my mind—an accordion and a balloon. Neatly sliced bread looked like an accordion, and when I picked up the bag, it felt like a balloon. I tried but never could appreciate this Wonder Bread stuff. Thanks to the many other types of bread baked in specialty stores and better bakeries, I did manage to find some bread to eat and came to enjoy it very much.

When summertime came, I couldn't adjust to air conditioning. Outside it was like an oven, and inside, like a refrigerator. I especially hated air conditioning in cars—it was freezing in there! However, after a few summer seasons I learned to greatly appreciate this American "necessity" of life, and now I am a true air-conditioning convert.

I loved teaching at the Missionary Training Center in Provo from day one. For me it was a blessing and a privilege from our Heavenly Father to help the newly re-established Czech mission by teaching young American missionaries and preparing them to enter my homeland. It was the most enjoyable job I had ever had in my life, and my very first opportunity to work for the Lord openly without fear of prison or constant pressure to hide my religion from the world. I cannot describe how much it meant to me just to walk through the MTC halls and see missionaries studying their scriptures publicly or carrying their religion handbooks and other supplies as they walked out of a building. I saw the same spiritual openness at the BYU campus, and my eyes were in tears the first few weeks. That's the spirit of freedom, I thought—to be engaged in good doings and not to be worried about the consequences. It affected me deeply.

I sat in one of the MTC hallways and watched the missionaries passing by. I just couldn't stop looking at their radiant, vibrant faces shining with excitement toward their future two years of service. I looked around and knew that I was at a place where most young Czech members would love to be. We younger members always heard so much about the American missionaries who had come and served in my homeland before the war. But we didn't know exactly what a missionary was, or what they looked like, because we had never seen them in Czechoslovakia. We were the only missionaries we knew! We had served as missionaries to each other during the years when the Church was not publicly acknowledged in Czechoslovakia, all of us working without any training.

I knew some of the stories about American missionaries by heart because some of the older members could never forget those who brought them to the gospel decades earlier. In the MTC I closely watched these young men and women and saw something I had never seen back in my country. Though they looked young, their faces radiated a certain feeling of mature confidence which came from their faith in the Lord. I looked at them and felt that the faith of these young people was deeply rooted in Christ, although they didn't have so much of life's experience that comes with age. They were beautiful human souls, and I had the feeling that Heavenly Father would be well pleased with these good young people.

"This is just the best place to get ready for life," I told one of my friends on the phone. "There is no better place for a young man or woman to enter into a meaningful, happy life as an adult." As I taught students, I learned that it was not easy to stay two months at the MTC, learn a new language, and make all the other necessary preparations for a mission. It was a place for very hardworking, disciplined individuals, and for most of the young people, this was a real transition. I could tell after a couple of meetings with a new missionary group who these young people were and what kind of families they had and how sincerely their families lived the gospel. Many of them struggled because they realized what hard work they were going to begin and they weren't quite prepared mentally—or sometimes physically—to adjust to it. They were very tired, because their program was scheduled to the minute, from early morning to late in the evening. It was wonderful to see the good influence of those young missionaries in a group who had strong, solid testimonies of the gospel. These hardworking young people were able to transfer their radiant spirit to the rest of their class. I also realized that for some young people, reading the Book of Mormon was a task which they completed for the first time in their lives at the MTC.

I witnessed several cases in which a missionary's parent was going through a very serious illness and the missionary didn't know if he or she would see the parent again after serving a mission. I felt that to leave home and go on a mission under such a unique circumstance was evidence that great faith in God and a strong gospel education throughout childhood can create a strong, mature individual, able to carry responsibilities and jump the hurdles of life in a noble, humble, and Christlike manner. These young people became the youngest heroes on earth in my eyes. I saw their tears as they shared their testimonies, and I could feel the most beautiful spirit in their sincere prayers. They taught me what it meant for them to lean upon Christ with all of their hearts and minds. I wondered if I would stay or go on a mission in such a tough family situation. Most would probably stay home. I realized that through the close contact a missionary had with an ill parent through weekly letters, praying for them every day, and fulfilling all of a missionary's daily spiritual tasks, they were actually able to build a powerful personal connection that would last in their hearts for the rest of their lives. Their missionary service became an example for the rest of the missionaries. When I went back to Czechoslovakia I learned that these missionaries were often the most hardworking and happiest ones.

On a few occasions, I taught a missionary who struggled to keep up with all the necessary preparation and work. The schedule was too tough for an individual who wasn't used to a precisely planned time scheme, scheduled daily events, and regulated activities that provided a great deal of new information and required a lot of self-discipline. I observed that it was a place where a teacher as well as a student had to learn how to think more about others than himself or herself. To go through such a transition with all the missionaries was the most amazing experience I had at the MTC. For some missionaries, that transition was truly a painful process because the body was weak and the spirit needed to be awakened. For those whose minds were prepared for missionary work from their childhood, this time in their lives represented a truly joyful entrance into their spiritual adulthood. Therefore, there were differences among young people coming to the MTC. But though the young people arrived in various degrees of readiness for their MTC experience, I cannot remember one missionary who, after two months of training, wasn't ready to leave for a mission or did not understand the purpose of the work. Those who struggled the most were sometimes the finest missionaries when I later met them in the Czech mission field, and I marveled greatly at not only how much they had improved in speaking the Czech language but also at what mature missionaries they had become.

My time at the MTC was one of most marvelous blessings that Heavenly Father gave me in the United States—indeed, in all of my life up to that point. It was almost like being on my own mission. I was just as homesick as my students at the MTC were. I struggled with a second language as they did, and I also learned, as they did, the true meaning of missionary work and membership in the Church, as well as gaining a personal testimony and getting into the habit of daily scripture study. I went through a transition similar to theirs. The gospel which I had accepted a few years previous gained a new meaning to me, as I really felt a part of true Church work in a free country among free citizens and could breathe the gospel doctrines in like fresh air, openly, without being pressed or limited by anyone. It was altogether a new awakening to me. I saw the Church from an angle of reality which I had not been able to see before. I found a new meaning in my membership as I learned that The Church of Jesus Christ of Latter-day Saints is a very hard-working church and that the focus of the hearts and minds of the leaders is on building the kingdom of God.

I was just amazed at how well the MTC was organized. There wasn't anything in the entire program that seemed to lack a clear direction or God's inspiration. As a matter of fact, I was always positively surprised at the kind of changes that were happening for better preparation and teaching of the missionaries. It was a place of constant change from good to better. I loved that. It prevented everyone who participated from routinely or casually fulfilling their goals.

I always felt that a prayerful attitude was the most important part of any gathering I attended at the MTC. There was always something to learn that witnessed to me that God's inspiration worked at this place among all the teachers and leaders. Of course, if I wanted to find a negative thing or less-than-sterling behavior of a missionary, I could see that, too, but I didn't search for that. The MTC wasn't meant for that purpose. Rather it was designed for the opposite: it definitely helped every young man and woman who was sincere and humble to become a great young person, a wonderful example for the rest of his or her family, friends, fellowmen, and the citizens of the missionary's assigned country.

To me, an Eastern European who grew up among government leaders who didn't care about the spiritual wellness of the younger generation, it was an amazing miracle to see a missionary program with young nineteen-year-old men and twenty-one-year-old women who had decided to stop their studying and daily pleasures of life, leave their families and friends for two years, and go labor for the Lord. I really admire the young elders and sister missionaries of the Church and respect them as the most self-disciplined young people I have ever met.

17

LONG-DISTANCE LOVE

The Missionary Training Center was involved in one of the most significant events in my life, one which would lead toward yet another change in my future. Carol Hawkins arranged an interview with *BYU Today* (as it was then known), the monthly alumni magazine of the university. I was interviewed in the lobby at the MTC. I had been in the United States only two months at that time, and I was still struggling greatly with English. This interview took about four hours, and its purpose was to introduce me to many of those who would be attending the upcoming BYU women's conference in the Marriott Center in April 1991. I didn't know exactly how many people would read my story in the magazine or whether they would even be interested in reading about someone from an enemy land controlled by a Communist government. I just didn't have any idea what Americans really thought about a country like mine.

After the next *BYU Today* issue came out, I was surprised to find dozens of letters in my mail every day from all corners of the United States. I could hardly believe people's reaction. Many of them called me a hero. I couldn't understand why and didn't know what this word really meant in this country. Up to this point, I had always associated heroism with some Russian soldier who had come to "liberate" Czechoslovakia at the end of World War II or with some Communist who had done something ordinary but whose actions the state propagandized as being almost superhuman. There were so many in Czechoslovakia who were called heroes but who we knew to be simply Communist liars. The word *hero* was therefore so separated from its true meaning and so much put in a context of lies and cheap political gain that it felt funny to think of anyone connecting my name with this concept. From my Eastern European perspective, I understood that American people recognized and saw something unusual in my life, yet I still felt puzzled while seeing the written word *hero* in their letters. It felt either too strong a term or too funny.

One day in March 1991 I received a letter that caught my attention. It came in an overnight-delivery package to the MTC. I entered my classroom and saw on my desk a big blue envelope with an eagle symbol on the front.

Someone is really in a hurry here! I thought as I opened the big envelope. Inside there was a smaller envelope with a typed letter:

> I hope that this letter does not get your hopes up for some sort of very important correspondence, owing to the fancy overnight envelope in which it is arriving, but I hope that you will have a spare moment to read it just the same. I should warn you that perhaps you have not received a letter like this before.

I started reading and found this person's writing style very interesting. The letter felt somehow European to me, with its content as well as its ideas. The man who wrote the letter had learned a lot about my homeland as a young man, through his trombone professor at Florida State University. I read the following paragraph a few times and the words caught my close attention:

> When the Czech Philharmonic was on tour, I drove with my professor to various cities around the United States to spend some time with his Czech old friends. Naturally, some

of this fascination for the Czechs rubbed off on me. I am now a big fan of all the composers: Janacek, Dvorak, Martinu, Smetana, Suk, etc., and always found something special there in the phrases from this land. It was always an aspiration of mine to go to Prague and to see the beauty of the city for myself.

I wondered, What kind of person is this man if he feels about Czech music and the capital the way he writes? As I read the other lines, I learned that he had actually driven in a Trabant (the famous East German car made from fiberglass and having a two-stroke engine) from Leipzig to Prague.

He must have an extraordinarily adventurous spirit to do something like that, I thought as I read those lines; only someone who has driven a car like a Trabant could know exactly what endurance means. The Trabant is small and unbelievably slow, with no air conditioning, and it produces a lot of noise around you as well as a lot of smog behind you. It's uncomfortable for any kind of traveling, not to mention a long trip from Leipzig to Prague. Wow! I went on reading:

> I am also a fan of the theater, and I first became acquainted with Václav Havel when a theater in Baltimore staged one of his plays. I was very impressed and from then on began to learn more about him and to follow his fate in Czechoslovakia. Since then I have read his letters, interviews, and have marveled at this man. When have we heard a world leader speak in this fashion in the last forty years?

This fellow, who didn't have any reason to study about my country or have ancestors in Czechoslovakia, was actually interested in a person like Václav Havel? It was a more-than-interesting thought to ponder. I decided to write him back, and within a few days I received a phone call from him.

"Hi. This is Randy Campora," he introduced himself. Well, at that time I was receiving many phone calls, and for a moment I didn't know who I was talking with. Randy sensed that and added, "from Baltimore. I wrote you a letter a few days ago and you wrote me back."

We had a really nice, comfortable, interesting talk on the phone, and when we were about to finish, he asked me if he could call me back sometime. I really enjoyed the telephone conversation and said, "Sure, I am the only one at home; and besides my school, work, many firesides, and preparation for the women's conference, I am a lone soldier in the field." His call had come exactly at the time when the Tanner family, with whom I lived, were in Brazil as John taught for one semester at a university there.

It was the end of March 1991 when I received Randy's letter, and it was the busiest time for me. I was attending English classes, teaching at the MTC, preparing for the BYU women's conference speech, and answering many people who were calling me about my giving talks at firesides. I was really tired and exhausted, but the hardest task for me was to prepare the conference talk. I struggled a lot. I was frustrated, hopeless, and stressed. I knew exactly what I wanted to say, but my English was in such an infant stage that I didn't feel I could say it adequately. I was so grateful when Brother Ed Morrell, whom I had met when he was president of the Austrian mission and was visiting Czechoslovakia, offered his generous help. He spent so much time with me, spending hours at his BYU office computer and helping me to prepare and translate all my ideas and put them on the paper. Having served a full-time mission in Czechoslovakia as a young man, he understood Czech very well, and therefore our cooperation could flow freely. Without his help I wouldn't have been able to be prepared in the way I wanted. Best of all, he prepared a tape on which all the words were correctly pronounced. He was a real angel, and his hours of help showed me how much love he had for the Czech people. He represents to me an extraordinary picture of a missionary who serves in a country but never forgets about the people, letting them become a constant part of his heart and treating them as his extended family. That kind of love for people from a different country somehow penetrates all his life blood, and whenever there is a need to do something for the people he has learned to love and serve, he embraces the moment the best way he can. Ed Morrell helped me prepare for an unprecedented event in Czech Church history: my talk represented, for me at least, the very first time that a Czech member could address a large American Latter-day Saint audience and share the story of our people. I was so grateful for the love Brother Morrell had for my Czech fellowmen, which he manifested through his uncounted hours of helping me to be well prepared.

It was a miracle to me that I could do it. The first time Carol Hawkins, who was in charge of the program, took me to the Marriott Center, I just hoped that she wasn't serious when she said in the middle of the huge hall, "This is the place where you will speak. What do you think?" I thought that I might speak to a few hundred people, but it never crossed my mind that the number could come to thousands at a time.

"How many people will be here?"

"I don't know—probably a few thousand."

"Excuse me?"

"Yep," she said, seeing my surprise, and gave me a big bear hug.

"Well, Carol, I love you and admire you for the faith you have. I must go home and practice."

"Don't worry, Olga. I know you will be great!"

I had been in the United States for only four months, and speaking English wasn't at all natural to me yet—it was a great struggle—and I had just a week or so to prepare to speak in front of thousands! When I look back at this event in my life, I see it as a miracle. I wouldn't have thought back in Czechoslovakia that within four months of my arrival in the United States, I would be able to deliver a speech in the Marriott Center to such a large audience. I surprised myself most of all.

I had never witnessed a women's conference before and couldn't picture in my mind how it would be organized. The pulpit I was supposed to speak from was the largest one I have ever seen in my life. When I came to the stand during the women's meeting, I could hardly see the end of the seats in the hall, which were filled with people up to the top. It was wonderful to be surrounded by the Relief Society General Presidency and General Board. They were all so supportive, loving, and caring.

While Sister Carol Madsen was introducing me as the next speaker, I was still wondering how I could do it, but I knew that it was a reality which was about to happen. I sat quietly, praying in my heart. I knew I had done everything that I could possibly have done to prepare myself for speaking English. Slowly, I felt all my fear and uncertainty melting away, and I received the assurance of the Spirit that this whole experience was planned and approved of by the Lord and language wouldn't be a barrier. It came to me that what was important was the message and sincerity behind the language, and I knew that people would be able to feel it.

When I started speaking, I realized what a great blessing and a privilege Heavenly Father had given me to be able to share my testimony, life experiences, and all the different things I had faced as a Church member in Czechoslovakia, with the American sisters sitting in the hall that evening. I experienced a sudden, beautiful feeling of a running history through my blood and spirit. For the very first time in my life, I spoke to a large audience and was able to share with them, without fear, pure truth from my life as a Latter-day Saint. I didn't have to choose different words in my talk but could speak pure reality. Neither did I have to be afraid that afterwards policemen would take me to prison or pronounce me insane, as the Communists had often done in my homeland with religious people who would try to speak in public about their faith.

To experience such a dramatic episode in my personal life was a new opening to my heart and released some kind of inner chains which had restricted and limited my tongue and my heart during all my previous life.

My throat was pretty dry by the end of my speech, but that was the only unpleasantness I experienced that evening. Afterwards I met with many sisters from different places in the United States and found out that many of them had ancestors in my homeland. It was the most beautiful and happy evening in the United States for me so far, and I thought, I have never received so many hugs in my whole life.

Before the conference I had been speaking at a lot of firesides in Utah, but afterwards the invitations grew as fast as mushrooms after a good rain. I could have been speaking somewhere every day if I had agreed to it. It was a great opportunity to share my experiences, but it was physically very exhausting. Within a month I found myself worn out. It wasn't possible to go to school in the morning, teach in the afternoon, and then travel in the evening to a fireside. However, I didn't know if it would be polite to just say no. I felt I had been invited to come to the United States for this purpose and that was why the Lord brought me.

Thanks to a wonderful friend, Mark Austin, whom I had met in Czechoslovakia just a year before I came to the United States, I was sometimes able to relax while I was living in Provo by participating with many of his wonderful friends at BYU, going on weekend trips or to parties with them. When I told Mark what my schedule was like after the women's conference, he said, "You are going to collapse any day now. You cannot live at such a high speed." He considered helping me by being my "fireside manager" if I couldn't say no to the invitations, but I greatly appreciated his advice and, because of it, was able to change my hectic schedule for the better. I reduced my speaking engagements to just once a week, sometimes twice a week, instead of four times as I had been doing before.

It was always a unique experience to speak at a fireside. People had questions that showed me how much the "Iron Curtain" between the East and West had damaged our mutual perspective as nations and people.

"Do you have sugar in Czechoslovakia?" they would ask. "Do your children go to schools?" "Do you have hospitals?" "Do all the men in your country wear military uniforms?" "Was everyone a Communist in Czechoslovakia?" I felt like either laughing or crying as I responded to these questions. "Yes, we have sugar and hospitals, children go to school, men don't wear uniforms, and only a very small number of Czech people were Communists." But there was more behind these questions.

I was many times lying on my bed after coming home from such a fireside, unable to sleep. I would be thinking how the limited circumstances in my country had meant a limited information channel for the rest of the world, and I realized that people looked at us from angles I would never have imagined back in Czechoslovakia. My family never liked Communists, and I could say the same thing about the majority of the people I met in my homeland. But it had never crossed my mind that in a general world point of view, every Czech person was counted as a Communist simply because he or she lived there. I had a hard time with this attitude! It was sad and very depressing—but I understood. Some of the people were amazed that I survived in Communism, and I was amazed at how the gospel could be found in two different political entities that were for a long period of time the strongest and most dangerous enemies to each other. How easily we could stand against each other as nations on one hand and yet, on the other hand, feel an amazing unity as brothers and sisters in the gospel. This thought had never hit me so strongly until I was

in immediate contact with American people and we talked about
all the hard times from the past.

The firesides turned out to be a great education for me. I
learned more about my nation and people, in some ways, than I had
while living in Czechoslovakia. It was a new discovery to see my
life and my country from someone else's perspective. I met some
who had Czech ancestors and yet hated the country and others who
loved it deeply. However, there was one main difference between
these two groups. Those who disliked Czechoslovakia were the
young generation who had defected to the United States. The others, who loved their homeland and wanted to have contact and discover anything possible about the country of their ancestors, didn't
feel the burden of the sad Czech history as did those who had left
Czechoslovakia before or during the Communist years because of
some kind of persecution. When I had a chance to talk to some
Czech immigrants to the United States, most of them would speak
harshly and with a certain disdain about Czechoslovakia. I understood this, but I was and still am always grateful to find a Czech in
the United States who would recall the positive side of the country
instead of seeing everything thorough a dark filter. I think I understand why some people wanted to forget their homeland, because
I myself felt many times embarrassed, frustrated, and even angry
when my eyes were opened to the greater privileges of life in a free
America—the ability to do simple things like withdrawing money
from a cash machine on a street, writing a check in a store, or just
walking comfortably and confidently through a store where almost
each item was a new discovery. I hardly knew how to deal with
these simple freedoms so new to me and yet a natural, basic, casual
"necessity of life" for any American.

But this kind of frustration generally created in me not a strong
resentment but rather an overwhelming pressure regarding material
things that surrounded me and that I had not yet had the chance to
take advantage of. At first I caught myself constantly comparing

Czech things and ways to those I found in the United States in
order to make some sense of it all. But I soon found that I needed to
accept this country the way it was and not make a constant comparison with my homeland. It was a hard lesson but necessary to
learn as soon as possible. It was sort of like the moment that you
realize you are thinking completely in a new language and not
thinking things first in Czech and then translating them into English
and then speaking the words. After a while, the language springs
from its own font, from a new place in your mind.

Randy Campora, the man who had contacted me with the
attention-getting letter just before the women's conference, called
on the phone at first only twice a week and later every day. We
became great phone friends. He was a great cultural guide, and we
had great fun on the phone just talking about some of my new discoveries in Provo. After a few weeks of talking on the phone
together, I had to admit to myself that I was impatiently waiting for
his phone calls each evening. Soon we felt like wonderful friends
although we hadn't yet seen each other.

"I was wondering, what would you say if we could meet each
other in person?" he asked in the middle of May, and he continued,
"I have been invited to a wedding in Utah, and I also have many
relatives I would love to see there."

"It sounds great. I like the idea very much."

There was definitely a chemistry in the air between us, but we
both were hesitant to speak too directly of this fact over the phone.
We were too careful. What if I feel so close to him on the phone
and when I see him I'm completely disappointed? I worried.

The plans were made, and we were supposed to meet in front
of a building on the BYU campus after classes. On my way out of
the building, I happened to meet one of my teachers, a really good
friend of mine, but she didn't know about my nervous meeting with
Sir Randy of the Phone. We chatted for a minute, and I saw out of
the corner of my eye a young man approaching us. He said,

"Excuse me, but I was supposed to meet Miss Olga Kovářová at 1:00 P.M." I replied, "That's me." My teacher discreetly disappeared, and I received a gentle and familiar hug.

We really had a great time that week as we visited many places and some of his relatives. It was really surprising to both of us how comfortable we felt with each other. It was like meeting a best friend after a long period of absence.

The world is so small. We drove that day over to the Tanners' house, where I lived. I invited Randy for lunch. He sat in the living room, looking at the photographs on the wall, and suddenly he said, "Do you know if these people lived in Florida at one time?"

"Yes, they have mentioned Florida a few times."

"Well, then, I know them. They were in my ward." I couldn't believe that the world could be so small. This connection actually became very important because when the Tanners came back from Brazil a few months later and I told them about Randy, they knew his whole family. Brother Tanner spoke highly of Randy, and he even remembered teaching him in a Church class. That was great news to me; a number of my friends were worried when I told them about a Mormon musician from Baltimore, but when they heard an exceptionally nice report from John and Susan, they were happy and smiling.

I visited Randy in Baltimore in August. He introduced me to beautiful places on the East Coast, and we also drove to see his family in North Carolina for a few days. His mother, Linda, embraced me like my own mom, and I didn't feel like a stranger but like someone who was fully accepted. We attended church at their ward, and after the meetings, a ward member congratulated us on our engagement.

"Well, we aren't . . . yet," Randy replied, his face turning red. After the Sunday meetings we went for a short walk in the park on the way home. It was a beautiful, sunny day.

"Well, I am really sorry for that lady's remark. I hope it didn't embarrass you," Randy apologized.

Actually, I didn't understand the real meaning of the word *engagement,* so for me the remark hadn't been a big deal since it had kind of gone over my head. I had only sensed that something was said which wasn't exactly proper, but frankly, I didn't know what it was.

"What was that lady saying?" I asked.

"She congratulated us on our coming marriage," he said, and I started smiling.

"Well, Olga, actually . . . there is a certain question . . . that I would like to ask you . . . when the right moment arrives."

I didn't even flinch, and I said, looking into his eyes, "I think that moment just arrived."

"Are you serious?" he asked.

"Yes, I am."

"Well do you think this place is decent enough to ask you the question?"

"I think it's fine!"

"Well," he continued, "I don't have any flowers, no ring, and the mariachi band is not hired yet!"

Right then and there Randy asked the Question and I gave him the Answer, much to the delight of the joggers passing by. Although we were surrounded by joggers and walkers that Sunday afternoon on the path under the North Carolina pines, we both have treasured this as one of the most beautiful moments of our lives together.

We knew at the time that it would be hard to be apart and to make all our wedding preparations by telephone, divided by thousands of miles. I had a chance to come to visit Randy once before the wedding, but other than that, we actually never officially dated each other. How strange I would think it if someone told me a story like that! But I knew that marrying Randy was right for me. I had really been thinking about him before our engagement, and I had asked Heavenly Father many questions. I felt strongly about our relationship, but I also knew that if we fell in love and were married, it would mean a major change in my life, not only because I would become a married woman but also because I would actually permanently separate myself from my homeland and live in a different country with different a language, far away from my family. Was it right? I felt so peaceful in my heart from the first time I asked Father the question that it was almost as if Heavenly Father was telling me, "You know very well yourself what my answer is, so just go ahead!"

When we got home to Randy's mother's house, we pretended nothing was going on and had a good laugh at the well-meaning ward sister who had jumped the gun on our engagement. Then we told Randy's mom the news. It was such a powerful moment for both of us, and she was overjoyed.

I called my parents in Czechoslovakia after the engagement. When my mom answered the phone, I said, "Hi, Mom, I have news for you. Guess what it is?"

"You are getting married."

"How do you know that?"

"Because I am your mom." Well, she knew a lot about Randy from my letters, and my voice was probably so excited that it wasn't hard to figure out that something extraordinary had recently happened in my life.

"How do you feel about it?" I asked my mom.

"You know that we always trust your judgment, and President and Sister Winder told us wonderful things about Randy." (Sister Winder had met Randy's mom on a Relief Society trip to Florida.) "We thought about it a lot," she continued.

"Are you happy for me?"

"Yes, very happy."

"Even Dad?"

"Yes, we both are happy for you." These sentences meant so

much to me! I knew that my parents faced a challenge they probably never had thought about, with their only daughter planning to live in the United States instead of Czechoslovakia.

"Olga, we cannot afford to come to your wedding, you know that, but we want to let you know that we love both of you and will be waiting for you to come to visit us in the future," Mom said with great emotion. She always thought about things in advance.

"But Mom, I think we can manage it. You could come."

"Olga, you know it would mean a lot of complications to obtain visas in such a short period of time, and we've never flown before."

"What do you want me to do?"

"We want both of you to come after your wedding to see us in Czechoslovakia."

"Well, do you really both feel comfortable about it?"

"Absolutely. We already thought about it."

I talked with Dad. He said, "Don't worry—we will be with you in the temple in our thoughts and prayers."

When he hung up the phone, I knelt down and prayed to know again that this was really right. I saw both of my parents and felt their hearts, their love and care for me. They always acted humbly and honestly, and I knew they didn't speak their opinions without thinking situations through first. Indeed, although it was a very unique situation for me, I felt peace in my heart and knew that taking into account all the circumstances, my parents had made the right decision. I realized that they would need more time to prepare themselves physically and mentally for the trip than we had time for. I thought about their decision many times, talked about it on the phone with them, and finally realized how much they loved me. Though distance divided us, I didn't feel separated from their love and ongoing concern for my well-being.

"Olga, we are sealed together for eternity, and that's what

matters, right?" my dad asked, and I could feel his strength, love, and vision.

One of the most wonderful experiences of our courtship was to introduce Randy to my parents by telephone, with me serving as a translator. There was so much mutual understanding and love among the four of us that I knew the connection was approved in the heavens. It was important to all of us to feel this spirit-to-spirit communication even though physical distance was so great.

On December 6, 1991, President Thomas S. Monson performed our wedding ceremony in the Salt Lake Temple. President Monson had known Randy's grandparents, Earl and Mildred Mendenhall, when they were serving a mission in New Zealand some years ago, and he also had met me during his trip to Czechoslovakia. During the wedding ceremony, as Randy and I looked at each other, if felt to me as if, for a very brief moment, all of the eternities dropped what they were doing and focused on us. It seemed as though there were heavenly choirs singing for us—choruses made up of family members who had passed on and some who were yet to come to earth because of our decision to be sealed in the temple of the Lord for all eternity. I felt as if we were the focus of a loving Father's full attention, in the company of our family and friends who were with us that day in his holy house.

A new life began for both of us—and, for me, also the reality of my life in the United States. I knew only the American-Mormon style of life so far. How different would life be on the East Coast? I wondered. I knew I would be surrounded by people of many nations, cultures, and life values, and I realized that the majority of my neighbors would either be members of other denominations or people with no religion. What would be their life attitudes? I was about to find out, and I looked forward to every minute of it.

18

A Tree Transplanted

During my first year in Baltimore, I literally felt like a transplanted tree, with its roots in foreign soil. I found it quite a challenge to be, first, a stranger in a new country and city where I would never have dreamed I would live in my life and second, a newlywed—an altogether new state of being after thirty years of single life.

Except for my husband, Randy, I didn't know one soul in Baltimore. While experiencing this metamorphosis, I felt a mixture of real happiness and deep homesickness. There was only one good medicine and I knew it—patience. It would take time and a good attitude to become a growing and giving person again.

The worst mistake I made was that I created what I would call a language prison. My daily conversations in stores, at gas stations, at the dinner table, and everywhere else were peppered with phrases like "Excuse me?," "What does that word mean?," "What did you say?," "Pardon?," "I am sorry—I don't understand," and "Could you repeat it again?" My personality went through a real self-confidence check. I developed a false fear that I couldn't express my thoughts in English in a natural way, as I used to do in my mother tongue, and this limitation made me feel like a half-person. Although people around me didn't see it that way at all and always sincerely complimented my English, I created this hurdle in my mind and couldn't get rid of it for a long time. I had never experienced such a thing before.

The more I concentrated on dealing with English, the less confident I felt with the language. I was ashamed to speak and ended up only halfway finishing my thoughts. I appeared to myself to be suddenly a very serious person, so caught in a language barrier that I was unable to make any jokes. I cried and was often angry with myself. It was the wrong attitude and I had to change it—I knew that. However, it took me a good amount of time to shake off this language beetle in my mind that was bugging me greatly.

Gradually I came to realize that it was my ego which suffered the most. I learned this when I talked for the first time in the sacrament meeting in Baltimore. I had a great topic to speak about— Easter. While I was speaking, I suddenly and strongly felt the Spirit of the Lord testify to me that I was fluent and free in my new tongue and all my language worries stemmed only from a mistaken attitude. This flash of inspiration came as quickly as lightning from the sky, but I have never forgotten what I learned while giving that talk. I found that among people there is only one important language that helps us to understand each other fully: the language of our heart, which is the language of love and of the Spirit of God.

I loved marriage from the first minute. It was a great change in both of our lives. Since we didn't have a chance to date each other before our marriage, we enjoyed dating and getting to know each other in our everyday circumstances. Randy introduced me to many of his wonderful friends from the orchestra, who always treated me as a member of their musicians' family. They were masters in encouraging me to explore Italian pesto and eat delicious Maryland crabs and other kinds of seafood—including squid, which became my favorite. They taught me how to watch American baseball and how to actually enjoy it, and I explored new places near the Atlantic Ocean as we all shared vacations and hobbies. Because many of them were also of different ethnic and religious origins, I learned a great deal as we discussed our differing life paths. I felt rejuvenated and refreshed. They were an important part of my creating a new circle of acceptance and belonging with others.

There were many situations in which I had just to laugh and take it easy. On one of my first days in Baltimore, I went with Randy to a grocery store. Among other things, I needed to buy rice. Randy took me over to the right section of the store.

I couldn't believe my eyes. "This is all just only rice?" I asked.

"Yes," he answered. I just started laughing. There were probably at least fifty different kinds of rice.

"I am pretty sure you don't have the one I used to cook and eat in Czechoslovakia my whole life. Please, just pick one," I said. "I would have to sit down and study all morning the information written on the rice to be able to pick the one I needed."

"Oli, that's OK. It's just silly capitalism that you see, right?" Randy smiled and picked the first one on the shelf. He gave me a hug and we left the rice world.

I was so grateful for Randy's patience during the first two years of our marriage. He always took time to explain to me the basic elements of American life, and he did so with a great sense of humor. There wasn't once a situation in which he lost his patience or laughed at me because of my questions or my way of walking around someplace as lost as a porcelain elephant. His kindness was amazing to me, because I lost patience with myself many times during this period.

Although people spoke English in all parts of America, I had to learn that regions of the country can be quite different from each other in certain ways. Life in Baltimore was very different from life in Provo. From a safety point of view, living in Provo was like walking in an oasis of peace, and living in Baltimore was more like walking among hungry lions. If I would leave a car unlocked in Provo, when I returned to the car, it would be just like I had left it;

but if anything like that would happen in Baltimore, I would be lucky if I found the car the next day. Randy needed to explain to me many times that the safety I was used to in my country or in Provo was not available in Baltimore. One evening several years before we were married, Randy was about to unload his groceries from the trunk of his car when he suddenly felt a rifle at his back. Two men took his wallet while pointing a .22 rifle at him, then left within a few seconds. It was a scary story to hear, and I realized I had to be careful and alert in my new environment.

It was challenging to deal with the immigration office as I completed all the processes necessary to becoming a resident of the United States. It was the very first time in my adult life when I was without a job, and I couldn't actually apply for any because of my visa status. Although I really didn't need a job, I felt very strange to be even temporarily unacceptable as a worker. Two things provided the greatest challenges to me—I wasn't used to living without working and also I was of course unaccustomed to life in America. During the process of applying for a visa, I spent hours waiting in a room with people from all nationalities, and many individuals showed an obvious desperation to belong to this country. Observing their anxiety, I wondered if I should be desperate, too. I also wondered, as I watched other immigrants, what brought them to the United States and why they were so determined to live here. I could readily tell the difference between those entering the first stage of the immigration process and those coming into the office to pick up a resident card.

I was filled with frustration and uncertainty as I went through this process. I had a literal feeling of belonging to the bottom of society in this huge country. There was something just slightly similar to a feeling I had back in Czechoslovakia while waiting for Communists to approve certain decisions I had made. I didn't feel the spirit of oppression in the United States, of course, but I nevertheless worried about government officials determining my future.

I tried to stay objective by reminding myself that obtaining a visa was just a necessary piece of a new mosaic of my life.

I tried to learn how to deal with the feeling of homesickness day by day. Some days were more successful than others. The most important fact for me was that I knew that I was in the right place, where I was supposed to be. Whenever a feeling of loneliness for my country came, I remembered feeling the Spirit strongly while praying about Randy as my future husband. I knew we had followed the inspiration of the Lord when we had taken this major step. This knowledge always gave me new energy, optimism, and desire to overcome strange new things.

I recognized in time that it was my responsibility to create and discover happy experiences in my new environment. There were so many beautiful memories inside my heart from my homeland, but I needed to recognize new opportunities and create brand new beautiful memories tied to my new environment. I learned that it is important to take a positive and creative approach and to have a solid daily schedule. Especially helpful to me was to walk in places where I could see trees, flowers, houses, and streets and then return there the next day and try to find beauty and begin to build the feeling of a new, growing familiarity with and belonging to the new area. It was a new school of life for me. I was actually grateful that I had time to sit down on the grass and watch nature around me and listen to different and unfamiliar sounds of nature.

Although I always got compliments on how well I spoke English, I knew the real story was somewhat different. I had a desire to continue English classes and improve my writing skills as well as my English vocabulary. Randy helped me to find and enroll in a few classes which kept me busy. It turned out to be a great decision; I enjoyed being a student again and enjoyed learning a new language that would be the mother tongue of my children. I realize I will never completely erase my Czech accent in my English; it was and is a stamp of my belonging to my ancestors in the Czech Republic. But I just wanted to make sure that people could understand me. I took comfort from wise words I had earlier heard from a family I had visited when I was still in Utah. They had a lot of visitors, and among them was a man who spoke with accented English. The kids made funny remarks after the foreigner left the house. The children's mother told them, "If you hear someone speaking your language with an accent, I want to you to think about something. It means that he or she knows at least one more language than you do! So what is so funny about that? Americans are sometimes ignorant of other languages, and when we make fun of someone's foreign accent, we really aren't being so smart and entertaining as we think."

If there was a place or people where I felt most comfortable during my first years in Baltimore, it was the Church and its members. The ward we belonged to was very unique in that it contained members from a wide cross-section of Baltimore. I met all kinds of people: some were medical students and doctors at Johns Hopkins University, some were only one bit of bad luck away from being homeless, some didn't know how to read and write, and some had problems with illegal drugs. Many nations and all different generations were represented. It was just a perfect ward of great diversity.

To that point in my life as a member of The Church of Jesus Christ of Latter-day Saints, I had had the experience of living in just two places where I attended the Church regularly: Utah and the Czech Republic. Besides that, I had occasionally visited wards in East Germany and Austria. Perhaps partly because my very first Church experience was in my homeland, I could feel the Spirit as strongly there as at any other place where Latter-day Saints gathered. I learned in the Church in my country to appreciate small and great miracles alike—things like sharing one copy of the Book of Mormon throughout the entire branch, being baptized in the lake in the middle of the night, and seeing every branch member share his or her testimony on fast Sundays. In East Germany I saw all the Church meetings start precisely on time, with things in great order, and with everyone knowing exactly where to go and what to do. In East Germany I admired the very first chapel I had ever seen. It was a meeting place officially built by the Church in Leipzig. In Vienna I had a chance to visit an American ward with many foreign students and military servicemen, and I felt for the first time freedom of worship as ward members openly met and learned of the Savior and his teachings. In my Provo ward, I had been amazed to see the biggest Primary class I had ever seen, together with the largest families on earth, learning beautiful Church hymns I had never heard before, feeling a reverent quietness on Sundays as the whole neighborhood kept the Sabbath day holy.

In my new Baltimore ward I found a great diversity, with many wonderful, bright, young couples starting their lives and families while studying at the university. I sensed the desire of many new converts to find and live correct principles despite the total lack of support around them, and I knew members struggling with poverty, drugs, unemployment, and illiteracy, not to mention bullets flying around their neighborhoods.

I was so impressed with the ward bishop, a native of Korea named David Chon, and his wonderful wife, Julie, and their seven daughters. He always stayed at the exit door of the chapel after sacrament meeting to greet and shake hands with everyone. I really felt welcomed into the ward. I will never forget a small but very meaningful experience I had with his wife, Julie, when I had been in Baltimore for only a month and was, in addition, sick with the flu. The phone rang and I answered. "Hi, Sister Olga, this is Sister Julie Chon. I am calling to ask you how you are doing."

I was really surprised to hear her voice and could hardly say a word. She continued to ask about my health, and I responded to her friendliness. We had a small chat together. This phone call meant the world to me at that time. I felt that someone cared for me and loved me. I was going through a period of intensely missing my family, especially my parents, and this small kindness and others like it were much more helpful to me than anyone ever knew.

In Baltimore and Washington, I really saw a different face of America. It was new and sometimes horrifying to me. I saw people sitting or lying on the sidewalk begging for money. Not only did I not know what to think of this but also I had no idea what to say or do. While passing them, my throat felt like a half-swallowed aspirin. I felt an urgency to act, but I didn't see that urgency in others passing by these poor individuals. Should I give them money, should I ignore them, or should I smile and just say hello? Were all of them so unable to find a way to get their life in order? I was confused when I read in newspapers that some of these beggars were so good at their "job" that they were able to make one hundred fifty dollars a day from begging. I couldn't believe it! Beggars represented the new, scary, and bitter face of life I saw around me. They seemed very much like physical prisoners of life. Back in Communist Czechoslovakia, I had seen only mental prisoners of life—those who became slaves of Communists because they had committed some kind of a mistake toward the law of socialism, and in order to survive they had to become liars and servants of the secret police and the political regime. Because I had come from a country without freedom to a country that values freedom as the highest importance of life, I often thought about beggars and wondered about their lives. I recalled a very old truth which I had read about but never had seen: even if a person lives in a free land, he can be wrapped in his own bondage and feel like a slave all his life; conversely, a person may be deprived of all his freedom, but no one can take his inner freedom, the freedom of his thoughts and soul.

There were other things I had to quickly learn in Baltimore. To board a bus in Provo had not been any trouble, but to do the same thing in Baltimore could present real danger. It was scary to see some of the people who were waiting at a bus stop there. Also,

Randy and I drove through some neighborhoods where I saw things I had never seen before: people hanging out on their porches from dawn to dusk, dirty streets with all sorts of garbage everywhere, and children—small kids or teenagers—running across streets. When I saw these children during the day, I wondered why they weren't in school; and when I saw even young children running unsupervised in the streets late at night, I could not figure out why their parents had not put them to bed yet.

Randy said, "Although it's hard to understand neighborhoods very different from our own, those people need the gospel more than anybody else." He was right.

After a few weeks of going to church in Baltimore, I received a calling as a Sunday School teacher for the sixteen- and seventeen-year-olds. I was more concerned with how I was going to teach lessons in English than I was with the age group, which everybody in the ward jokingly warned me about. It was a just a small group of seven teenagers, all of them from active ward families. I really enjoyed the calling despite the language and teenage challenges I faced in the class. The youth were really supportive of me, especially the girls. Whenever I messed up an English word, they would immediately come up with help. It was an interesting experience for both sides. The class was amazed to see a tiny-sized Book of Mormon in Czech or just to hear how Czech people were usually baptized during the time of Communism in my country. For me it was especially interesting to compare this group of young members to young people in my country. I didn't have the chance to see Czech teenaged members, since that age group was almost totally missing from small LDS congregations throughout the whole country. Therefore, I knew that I could learn much from this particular age group and their attitudes toward life and the gospel. I found it interesting and inspiring to see that these young people, although struggling with their age challenges, had great gospel values firmly rooted in their hearts. They seemed to me like any Czech teenagers, but the difference was in a knowledge of life values. Whereas most teenagers from my country didn't have any real values, these young American Church members had a rich storage of the right gospel principles.

19

GROWING SEASON

I experienced a new spiritual season in my life while moving to Baltimore as a married woman. When I lived in Provo, I felt almost as if I were there on a unique mission. My life was fully devoted to the work I was doing: teaching at the Missionary Training Center, speaking at the women's conference, translating for the general conference sessions, and speaking at many firesides. When I moved to Baltimore, I came back to a casual daily schedule. It was quite a big change. Suddenly, no one called me about speaking at firesides, and not only people outside the Church but also the members of the ward were unaware of my background. Baltimore seemed to have so many bizarre characteristics as a city, but I saw one point similar to my small hometown in Czechoslovakia: I lived among neighbors who were not members of the Church. Somehow that felt good; in Utah, I had found it hard to adjust to the fact that almost everyone I saw on the sidewalk, in a store, or at school was a member of the Church—either active or less-active. It had been very different to me to be surrounded by Church members, and for some reason I had really missed the challenge of having member-missionary opportunities all around me. I looked forward to being challenged again, this time in an American city.

I didn't realize how hard missionary work in America could be. Finding new ways of being a member missionary in the city of Baltimore was literally like exploring new spiritual gifts and talents that Heavenly Father has in his storage for us, reserved for the time when we wish to open them. I learned a new lesson—that there can actually be very beneficial missionary work inside the Church with less-active members or those who suffer from weak or lost testimony in their lives.

It was definitely hard to discuss religious topics with some of Randy's best friends. They would jump out of the discussion right as I was beginning it. But I loved to visit many members who had been less active for years and needed to feel loved, appreciated, and supported. Also, new converts needed so much attention to develop healthy gospel principles in their lives and homes. I found that I could greatly benefit from all the missionary work I had done and the knowledge I had gained as a Church member in Czecho-slovakia. I had developed a strong, positive life attitude during my years of teaching people about the gospel in Czechoslovakia, and I had gained a personal testimony of the joy of living the gospel, which was able to light people up with hope for their own lives. I found that my attitude of a deep appreciation for my membership in the Church had given me a foundation for growing into spiritual maturity and dedication to the Lord's work. It was in Baltimore that I realized that I was meant to be born in Czechoslovakia. I gained so much there, although through some pain. In my homeland I had gained a deep desire to be trained in the work of the Lord in order to become as good a servant of the Lord as possible. This sense of my personal spiritual path—trying to become more like Jesus so I could be more useful to him and more prepared to live with him— came from my growing up in a place few people would choose, Communist Czechoslovakia.

It was a relief and also a new level of spiritual understanding to come to such a knowledge. I learned to be grateful for America and for the inner spiritual freedom and understanding of my life that I obtained while living among people of a different background and language. My perspective of the place where I lived totally changed. I stopped comparing my homeland with the United States and started absorbing the beauty of life here in America. It took me about three years to come to this understanding. When I did, I felt as if I were coming from a high mountain covered in a heavy, milky fog and seeing myself in a real mirror of life again. Also, I found a new ability to see not only one tree and then another one but to be able to absorb the beauty of all the trees of life together as one large woodland. Randy was always reminding me of this, and with every new victory of happiness I felt while exploring something positive, he would encourage me and say, "That's another step towards coming out of the woods."

I was excited when we traveled to Czechoslovakia during the spring after we got married. My parents and family would finally meet Randy. We planned a family reunion, and because of that, I traveled to Czechoslovakia a few weeks earlier than Randy. I was returning after one and a half years of living in the United States. I was coming to my homeland, which had changed not only to a presidential and democratic government just before I had left, but also had taken on a new name during my absence. There wasn't a country called Czechoslovakia anymore. I arrived to two different lands—the Czech Republic and Slovakia. I found myself a citizen of the new Czech Republic. I smiled while thinking that the both of us—my country and I—had changed our status: I had received the new name of Campora and had stopped using Kovářová, and my homeland was now called the Czech Republic instead Czechoslovakia.

My country, as well as I, was creating a new personal history and going through transitions—both of us in different ways and a long distance from each other. I wondered how my family and my friends would feel, seeing me coming back to my homeland as a visitor. While leaving Czechoslovakia on my trip to the United States one and a half years earlier, this possibility hadn't crossed my mind.

It was really interesting for me to search the feelings inside my heart while visiting my country after a long absence. I felt like a different person. Somehow I didn't fully fit into the environment to which I had returned. My thoughts and life perspective were different and were connected with my new experiences in a country most of my countrymen just dreamed of visiting. My soul was shaped in new wave patterns. I spoke a different language, ate different food, had new friends, and felt a new understanding of the gospel. That was the most major change I felt, in fact. I came to the Sunday meeting and saw some familiar faces. My old friends were sitting in the same chairs where I would have found them two years ago, and they were asking the same questions I used to ask while teaching them in Sunday school a long time ago.

I had spent the first thirty years of life in my country seeing hardly any changes in the political or religious status of the land, and now that I was returning, I could hardly recognize the new face of my hometown or the other places I visited. The results of the 1989 revolution appeared quite visible to me. I saw great transitions taking place everywhere. Not only were the houses, stores, and streets undergoing this change, but the people I knew so well were also reacting and adjusting to all these huge reforms in their lives and environment. I found friends without work or about to lose their jobs, and I talked to some who were confused, critical, and pessimistic due to the new storms they were weathering. But I saw many who were becoming successful and finding a way to support their families. I also found a small group of young members who had become far too successful in the world and didn't know how to juggle their material success with their priesthood and Church responsibilities.

My hometown branch was undergoing a hard time. Leaders

were trying to find a location for a chapel but were not yet meeting with success, which was very discouraging for them. There were also other changes in the branch, including a higher percentage of inactivity. It was hard for some priesthood holders to see a new convert ordained a priest within months of baptism, when they had waited twenty or forty years for the same ordinance. It was challenging for others to see the open status of the Church working in public. Some missed the close, family feeling that had prevailed when meetings had been held secretly in Church members' homes.

I spoke at many firesides back in the Czech Republic about my experiences in the Church in the United States. I wanted to show concerned Church members that all the changes they were going through were for their good and that the sweeping governmental changes, including freedom of worship, were exactly what we had prayed for! A majority of the new members I met were young people, some of them even high school students. It was wonderful to see a new image of the Church. One branch met at a music school with a cold, uninviting atmosphere, uncomfortable chairs, and a physical lack of atmosphere for new investigators. Members and investigators alike may think it was kind of funny to make a sacrament table from a schoolteacher's desk. But the branch was involved in a process of growing, and to gain a better meeting place required members to grow in faith, stay faithful in keeping all God's commandments, and reach out to others.

I could understand some of the undercurrents of frustration among Church members in the new Czech Republic. I had found that precisely this stage was the most trying period of my own Church membership, even harder than just hiding myself from the secret police as we used to do before the revolution.

Also, because of the changes of life which came naturally with a new government—changes in work, family life, and financial struggles—some members found themselves struggling just to deal with the basics. Many of the members found good jobs that required working on weekends, which created problems on the Sabbath day. Many who were struggling financially found it difficult to reconcile the demands of family economy with the commandment to keep the Sabbath day holy.

However, I also met many old and new members who were radiating the Spirit, full of joy and energy, and happy to be working in the Lord's church. There was so much opportunity for them to share the gospel, and somehow they seemed to develop mature testimonies within a shorter period of time than had those of us who joined the Church during the incognito years. I believe these new members had a great advantage in seeing the Church functioning the way it was supposed to, instead of meeting secretly, with some important parts of the gospel missing due to lack of knowledge and lack of contact with Church headquarters. With Communist restrictions removed, local members could enjoy the full Church program. More new classes were opened in Czech branches, and more people got the opportunity to serve in many diverse callings. Among the newer converts were married couples and young families, and it was wonderful to see that the Czech Church had started to show a face of diversity. Before the revolution, a great majority of members were single or widowed. To the members of a small Czech branch, the opportunity to have a Primary class—even one made up of children of many different ages—was a choice new experience. Members enjoyed gathering together and talking about Jesus so naturally. I had never seen anything like that in my country before, and I felt that the new religious openness in my homeland was the greatest miracle I saw during my visit.

The greatest joys of my visit, of course, revolved around my family. When preparations for the family reunion were complete, Randy joined us. My parents loved him at the very first bear hug. Because of his work schedule, I had arrived in the Czech Republic two weeks earlier than he, so when he came into the Vienna airport, my parents could hardly stand the suspense as they waited for him to step off the plane. They wanted so badly to finally meet him. I think we caused a major traffic jam as we all hugged each other at the customs exit. It was an emotional few days for everyone— indeed, the whole visit was an emotional high for all of us. Randy and my parents practically beamed at each other as they shared stories about me and talked about the life we lead in America and all the events that had transpired. Everyone was patient with Randy's fledgling Czech language skills, and very appreciative that he had begun learning enough to be basically conversational.

At the family cabin we convened the tribe to officially "unveil" him. He had brought with him a second wedding band just for the occasion: it was a simple gold band bearing the inscription *na čas a věčnost, Randy*—"For Time and All Eternity, Randy." We sat around the campfire in front of the cabin one beautiful evening and recounted the story of our meeting, our courtship, and our wedding in the house of the Lord. Randy then presented the ring to me, which made the family feel part of the event even though it had already happened. He talked about the history of his family, Italian pioneers on one side (immigrants who joined the Church in the early 1900s) and Mormon pioneers who crossed the plains from Nauvoo on the other. His parents each had written letters to be read at the campfire ceremony. This was the culmination of the beginning of an eternal Campora-Kovář family bond, and we all felt it deeply as such.

Altogether, it was an amazing experience to be back in the Czech Republic. But also I realized that I couldn't ever be the same person I was before I left my country for the United States. Living in America had taught me to appreciate and see things from a different perspective. When I looked back at my life, I realized I couldn't ever be pure Czech again, nor could I become a pure American. The two cultures had blended in my soul and spirit and created a new person. My experience in the United States had blessed me with a new perspective of life. My eyes were opened to see, feel, and appreciate things I would never have appreciated just by living my whole life in my homeland.

I came away from my visit to the Czech Republic with an understanding that we can make a difference in our personal Church life without digging in a blind, intellectual way into Church doctrines, as I could see happening in my country and also in the United States. Rather, we should try to extend our arms to others, to live according to the great principles we can learn from our scriptures, to follow our living prophets, and to support our fellow Latter-day Saints in a friendly atmosphere of love and mutual understanding. We need to balance our thinking and our quest for gospel knowledge with an equally large amount of service to the Lord.

I have sometimes tended to study the doctrines of the Church deeply and to dig at them, so to speak, from all different angles. That tendency, due in large part to my growing up in an atheistic society, was my spiritual Achilles' heel during the time when I was first learning about the Church. I questioned many of God's laws and powers, and I had little or no understanding of the role of true service to God. My faith was too theoretical in the beginning, too dry and too intellectual. But when real challenges came into my life and I learned that I could lean on the Lord for support and strength, my perspective changed completely. I gained a new understanding of studying scriptures and began studying them because I had come to love them and wanted to apply them to my life in order to find new joy, instead of studying them only to dig a new hole of doubt or to play intellectual games. I am really happy that I learned to respect the balance between study and service.

CHAPTER

20

NEW JOYS
AND CHALLENGES

Back in Baltimore after our trip to the Czech Republic, Randy and I continued to be busy and happy in our home, our work, and our Baltimore ward. One afternoon I found a message from Bishop Chon on the phone. When I called him back, he asked Randy and me to come to his office next day.

"Well, Sister Campora," the bishop began, "we want to call you as our ward Relief Society president. What do you think about it?"

I was surprised, but I accepted the challenge. The bishop and Randy expressed their confidence in me. I felt I had been prepared for this change in my life; earlier that same day, I had received an impression that my Church calling would soon change, and I had felt that my new calling would be another opportunity to grow.

Our Baltimore ward was going through a period of growth and challenges. The ward was having baptisms almost every Sunday at that time, with the result that our congregation grew by at least five new members each month. In addition, the ward was scattered all over the downtown areas and included other areas of town too.

I knew it would be a great challenge to serve as a ward Relief Society president, but I also knew that the Lord always has a purpose when members are given new responsibilities. As I accepted my new calling, I immediately felt joy and peace in my heart.

When I looked at a long list of all the sisters in the ward and saw a number close to five hundred, however, I knew there was a great deal of work to do. To determine the real number of existing sisters in our ward was my first goal. It took some time, but it was a good feeling when we identified and verified that three hundred LDS sisters lived in our ward area.

Whenever I serve in a new Church calling, I always ask these questions in the beginning: What needs to be achieved in this work? How I can be a good instrument in the Lord's hands as I work toward these goals? What existing talents do I need to use in my new calling? What new talents do I need to learn, or ask the Lord to bless me with, in order to fulfill the calling? I prayerfully asked these questions and began my work. Naturally, I found challenges along the way. For example, when we Czech sisters were teaching Relief Society lessons in small branches in my homeland, we had a difficult time applying some of the lessons to our local conditions. It was the usual thing in Communist Czechoslovakia for mothers and women to work away from home, and they weren't at home with their children. The new Czech members sometimes struggled, therefore, to understand the importance of motherhood in the role of women. Interestingly, I found similar challenges in the Baltimore ward, where the majority of women were working outside the home and many were single mothers. I also learned that because of our ward members' diverse backgrounds, there was a great demand for learning essential principles of the gospel, coupled with basic principles of sound, responsible living. In our Relief Society meetings, we had much vivid discussion of topics like clothing, money loans, credit cards, and honoring parents.

In the beginning, I didn't know how members would accept

someone as a Relief Society president who was of a different nationality, who had moved to the ward only a year earlier, and who was relatively young in comparison with some of the other sisters in the ward. However, I was delighted to see that my ward sisters supported and encouraged me from the beginning.

In the harsh winter of 1993, one sister, a recent convert, froze to death in her house, and we learned only after her death that her home didn't have electricity. Another ward member, an elderly sister, died of injuries inflicted by her son, an alcoholic. These and other sad stories affected me profoundly. I was devastated as I considered this bitter side of America and particularly the tragedies faced by some members of the Church who suffered even in this land of freedom and plenty.

Randy and I grieved that winter when I had a miscarriage after about two and a half months of pregnancy. The winter became so harsh that we couldn't even leave our home. Schools were closed, and we couldn't get to work. The roads were frozen. We both felt like prisoners inside our house, just looking through our windows at the long icicles hanging from our roof. We held hands, hugged, and cried together, feeling homesick for both of our families so far away from us.

The year 1995, however, brought great joy into our home. I continued serving as the ward Relief Society president, and Randy was called to serve as a high councilor in the Baltimore Stake and later, in December 1995, to serve as branch president when our large ward was divided into two smaller branches.

For Randy and me, the highlight of the year was the birth of our son, Dominik, on August 11, 1995. He was a healthy, happy, shining, and beautiful newborn. Of course it was like a steep mountain climb for me to bring Dominik into the world. But how elated I was to feel the happiness and joy as I embraced him in my arms! "I want to be as good as he is!" was the very first sentence Randy uttered while holding his son for the first time. It's not difficult to imagine what happy and proud parents we both became. Every day, Dominik gives us a bright new opportunity to grow and deepen our testimonies of the gospel. To us he seems a perfect miniature of our Heavenly Father, reminding us of our royal origins. Our joy and fulfillment were equalled by the challenges and fatigue of first-time parenthood. But Randy and I feel that even if we accomplish nothing else in this life, we hope to earn the supreme "Red Badge of Parenthood" as we protect and guide our little one through his mortal life, in accordance with Father's plan. This alone will have made our challenges worthwhile. Forget yoga and the trombone—"Suffer the little ones to come unto me" is what it's all about!

Now I have moved forward to a different season in my life—a very essential one. I am a mother! I've accepted a calling that was routinely overlooked, ignored, unappreciated, and buried deep, along with many of life's greatest joys, in the Communists' cemetery for moral values. In Communist Czechoslovakia, the Communist school was your mother. Your real family was little more than a place to take a shower, sleep, and have a warm meal once in a while. In your family, you celebrated once a year an uncomfortably warm/cold Christmas, complete with everything but its true meaning. If you were a parent in Communist times, you got a higher salary, were pronounced a hero on TV, and even received a president's honor award in the Prague castle at the end of each year, with the title *Zasloužilý Pracovník*—"Rewarded Worker"—if you worked weekends and longer-than-normal hours, especially during holidays, instead of being with your family. There was no time to develop many family traditions for the majority of Czech families, and I had never heard in Czechoslovakia the phrase *family reunion.* There were no national holidays to honor fathers or mothers; there was only International Mothers' Day—a day on which Communist leaders staged a poor comedy of nonsense. How can a nation like that provide a foundation for a woman to be a good mother? I am grateful for the gospel in my life, for it provided the foundation I

need, and it has brought me strength, understanding, and love as I
have attempted to sort through the wrong traditions generated in
my nation during the evil rule of Communism.

In Czechoslovakia I always had one big worry while thinking
about my future family, which I thought would include children living under Communist oppression. For some reason I was always
filled with fear as I wondered how I would secretly teach my children the gospel. I couldn't picture succeeding in this mission, with
my children facing animosity against God outside my home even
as I tried to create a celestial environment inside. I am happy and
deeply grateful to the Lord that the Czech Republic, Slovakia, and
other Eastern European countries now have religious freedom.
Newborn children in these lands have a choice that was forcefully
stolen from their parents and grandparents for many decades. I
want to hope that these choice children will have parents who will
sacrifice whatever it takes to build a strong family, which will in
turn make better nations and a morally clean world.

I believe that every person who makes an important difference
in some man's or woman's life toward good is deeply treasured by
the Lord. I also believe that those who bring up children in the light
and truth of God will be able to grow at the speed that was origi-
nally designed for us. When we teach our children eternal gospel
truths and live as examples of righteousness, we become the most
healthy, happy, and productive children of God we can be during
our mortal probation. For those who live the gospel and "endure to
the end," I believe the end of the mortal sojourn will be a happy
jump from earth to an eternal home.

The blessing of my somehow finding, in the dark days of
Communist rule, the light of the gospel of Jesus Christ remains a
miracle in my life. The president of the Czech Republic, Václav
Havel, eloquently described Communism's destructive influence
in a speech that I heard him give at George Washington University
(where I now teach Czech language classes) as he accepted an

honorary degree. He said, "Communism was far from being simply the dictatorship of one group of people over another. It was a genuinely totalitarian system; that is, it permeated every aspect of life and deformed everything it touched, including all the natural ways people had evolved of living together. It profoundly affected all forms of human behavior. For years, a specific structure of values and models of behavior was deliberately created in the consciousness of society. It was a perverted structure, one that went against all the natural tendencies of life, but society nevertheless internalized it, or rather was forced to internalize it" (Václav Havel, unpublished address, 1993).

It's a miracle to me that the Lord blessed me with the gospel in the midst of Communist Czechoslovakia's moral abyss. I consider the experience of my early membership in the Church in my homeland as the most unforgettable time of my life, as well as the joyful and sincere beginning of my faith's path. Czechoslovakia was the place where I first felt the Spirit of the Holy Ghost and received answers to my prayers about the truth of the restored gospel. It didn't matter that the circumstances around me reflected animosity, even hatred, toward God; that my parents didn't know too much about religious matters; or that all Czech schools and teachers taught me just the opposite of the truth about God's existence. My experiences in the gospel healed me and, most important, taught me that God speaks to people everywhere. It was marvelous to learn this. I felt a new inner freedom growing within me as I learned in Communist Czechoslovakia that no fence, not even the Iron Curtain, can limit God, and no enemy can stop his glorious work from unfolding as it should.

I am grateful to a small, shining, faithful group of Czech Saints who survived those dark years and nourished their spirits as best they could. Though their religious freedom was smothered, these old Czech Latter-day Saints found enough spiritual air to breathe their prayers and maintain hope in their lives. They found living water to quench their spiritual thirst. I was happy to meet them, to become a part of them, to be acquainted with them, and to serve as a small first evidence of the fruits of their remarkable underground missionary work. I remember some faithful Saints who, whenever they saw me after my baptism, said the event had brought them energy and a growing hope that there was ongoing life and forward motion in the Church in Czechoslovakia. A few of the older members told me that I, along with other young Czechs who joined the Church shortly after me, represented to them the joyous news that the Lord had not forgotten about them and their country. Later, when many other young Czech and Slovak people joined the Church, new converts found their place in the midst of the stalwart older Saints and soon were called as young branch presidents, Relief Society presidents, and other branch leaders.

One of the fables told by the wonderful Russian writer Ivan Andrejevic Krylov reminds me of the patience, persistence, and victory of these Czech Saints. He told the tale of two blackbirds who were flying here and there and found a pitcher in which there was a little water, just at the bottom. However, the vessel was too narrow and tall for them to drink from it. They tried to break the pitcher or tip it over to gain access to the water, but without success. One bird flew away, annoyed and filled with anger. The second stayed and pondered. Suddenly the bird saw something; around the pitcher lay a lot of pebbles. The bird brought one pebble after another and dropped it into the pitcher. The water rose higher, and within an hour the blackbird drank and quenched his fiery thirst.

The good Latter-day Saints of the Czech Republic are like the ingenious blackbird who found a way to turn temporary defeat into victory. They helped me take my first tottering steps as a Christian. I felt predominantly an abundance of joy and happiness as I enjoyed wonderful and unique missionary opportunities in the Czech Church. I gained a stronger testimony every time I taught gospel principles during a yoga lecture or camp and every time I wrote an article promoting solid Christian values, even if the article appeared in the form of a Communist newsletter sent to Brno educators.

As a Church member in Communist Czechoslovakia, I felt I was one of many soldiers quietly fighting a war against the prevailing religious darkness in my country. To my view, it was a war that had a good ending. Now that my countrymen once again enjoy religious and civil freedom, I feel like a soldier who has gone to war and has now returned and retired because the war is over. I was greatly blessed on the "battlefront"—I could have ended up in prison for my beliefs if the Communist government hadn't failed in 1989. If they had had their way, the secret police would have gone fiercely after many Czech members, including me. But that wasn't the case.

During my early years of Church membership in Communist Czechoslovakia, I generally felt that I would be protected and that my life would be well in the end. I didn't know, however, and could not even imagine that just seven years after my baptism, the incredibly forceful Communist government would fall early one morning, just like the sun bursts forth unexpectedly in the middle of a rainy day in Florida, and a new opportunity for a meaningful life would suddenly rise up for all Czech citizens.

Now I am putting away my "warrior uniform"—gladly and with peace in my heart. The beauty of life is that every mission has a beginning and an end. There is a small pause, and then I am again given an opportunity to learn and grow—by becoming a mother, accepting a calling as a Relief Society president, or beginning another new task. At first I don't have any clue as to how to conquer my new challenges, about which I might feel either uncomfortable or overjoyed. But after many sincere prayers, I learn that I need only to press forward, trusting in the Lord, in order to open myself to new and higher possibilities. That's the Lord's way.

How much did I learn during my early Church membership in

those Communist times? A great deal. I grew in gratitude for the Lord's marvelous ways of bringing the gospel to any place where there are people with willing hearts to receive it. I was most grateful for my opportunities to teach the gospel among the Czech people. As I helped teach others, I came to understand a simple truth: if I don't study, I will not know the word of God, and I will become a confused and lost individual.

The most essential lesson I learned during my early membership was that I didn't have time to flirt with the gospel; I needed to live it as fully as I possibly could. I also learned that the gospel wasn't just another philosophical bent or a fertile ground for sophisticated contentions. I found out that any merely philosophical discussion about the gospel, without the Spirit, was a waste of time. I discovered that living the true gospel means doing good despite any pressure I might feel. I came to understand and appreciate the simplicity of the gospel. Starting to obey God's commandments has brought me on a journey of joy and has taught me the real meaning of freedom.

It is still amazing to me that I have planted my roots in this land where many of my Czech ancestors only dreamed to visit. How would they feel to know that I am here and that the very thing that brought me here was my acceptance of the restored gospel of Jesus Christ? Like them, I dreamed of touching America's ground and of getting a feeling of this beautiful promised land of freedom for myself. The dream I had merely imagined while traveling many times with my fingers on the world map above my bed in little old Uherské Hradiště became a reality when I found Heavenly Father, his true Church, and his plan of happiness. I truly believe that the United States of America has uniquely wide highways to human freedom. My desire is to pass on to all of my children and grandchildren the narrow way to Christ. I count that as the most important goal of my life, the number-one reason why I am here on earth: "Strait is the gate, and narrow is the way, which leadeth unto life, and few there be that find it" (Matthew 7:14). What true rejoicing it brings to Randy's and my hearts to know that Heavenly Father's plan and Christ's role in it will make it possible, with our faithfulness, for our family to be successful on this narrow earthly way and ultimately pass, one by one, through the veil to be individually "encircled about eternally in the arms of his love" (2 Nephi 1:15).

I am grateful to my Heavenly Father for my life which he has given to me. I am grateful for the opportunity to write about one special and wonderful season of my life. My experiences in learning of and accepting the gospel are a unique and significant part of my eternal journey.

I never thought I would have the chance to write about all this, much less in English. I am most grateful for those individuals and families in the United States who financially and spiritually supported my coming here and for those families who sacrificed comfort and made room for me in their homes, even letting me become a part of their families for a short or long time. These wonderful Saints represent the greatest blessing in my life, and they have nourished my spirit in a very profound way. I was blessed as I watched their Church activity on rainy days and during down-to-earth family home evenings as well as during their happiest times and wonderful family celebrations.

I know deep in my heart that I wouldn't have been blessed with all these miracles in my life without the many prayers of wonderful Latter-day Saints throughout the world and especially in free America. Blessed with the opportunity to live the gospel and express your religious beliefs daily, you prayed for freedom in my country—openly in your Church meetings and privately in your homes and hearts—for many decades. Your prayers were heard, and God blessed my country with a miracle—the miracle of freedom. Your prayers for worldwide missionary success made a difference in my life; I was blessed to meet Czech Latter-day Saints and to be baptized and led to the light of truth in the midst of my country's spiritual darkness.

May my story be an expression of thanks and appreciation of a simple fact frequently emphasized in our ancient scriptures and in the words of living prophets, seers, and revelators: miracles indeed happen.

Above: Olga Kovářová (at left) enjoyed associating with friends during her gymnasium (high school) years, but none of them seemed to have the answers to life's important questions. Below: Skiing is one of the many sports in which Olga excelled as a young girl.

Above: Olga and Brother Otakar Vojkůvka, the faithful Latter-day Saint who introduced her to the gospel, study together in his home, 1985.
Below: Olga (standing near center) radiated newfound joy as she taught her first yoga classes in her hometown of Uherské Hradiště in the mid-1980s.

Above: Brother Otakar Vojkůvka (at left), a motivating force behind the yoga camp program, was also an active participant. Here, he leads camp participants in song (Olga, near center of photo, faces camera).

Below: As instructor and director of a large yoga camp program, Olga (photographed at camp, 1989) helped many fellow Czechs to replace anger, fear, and anxiety with positive thoughts and Christian traits and values.

Above: During week-long yoga camps, Olga found opportunities to meet with small groups of yoga participants who were interested in finding answers to life's big questions.
Below: During Olga's temporary stay in the United States, Randy Campora introduced him-self through an express-mail letter that led to courtship, engagement, and, in 1991, marriage.

Above: Olga's father, Zdeněk Kovář, and mother, Dana, made their first visit to the United States when they traveled to see Olga and Randy in spring 1994.
Below: In the Czech Republic, Olga and Randy's baby, Dominik, got acquainted with his great-grandmother, Ludmila Dudešková (August 1996).

Olga, Randy, and their son, Dominik (April 1997).

INDEX